"*Sorrow makes room* ju ...
fresh ways to see God and new pathways that deepen the well of grace within, but not without the soul-wrenching river of tears we would do anything to avoid. Jeanne and Bob Arnold and their family know this and have turned their mourning into comfort and blessing for many others. Their book, Deep Sorrow, Surprising Joy, is a testament that God can take anything, anything at all, and make something good out of it."
--Wes Yoder, author of *Bond of Brothers*

"*Marcie, Bob and Jeanne's daughter, was a beautiful young lady with so much potential, like my daughter, Rachel. Then, without warning or preparation she was suddenly gone. This book is a brutally honest and compelling commentary on the journey that they traveled to achieve healing from the incomprehensible wound of losing a child.*
"*It provides a beacon of hope to anyone who has lost a loved one. It is also a compelling story for those who have not. Bob and Jeanne are two of the most wonderful people I have ever known, and you will learn much about how to live in grace and comfort through this book.*"
--Darrell Scott, author of *Rachel's Tears*

"*The stories told within these pages brought tears, healing, and hope as I read about the faithfulness of God in the midst of incredible pain. I am inspired by the courage of Bob and Jeanne to tell their story and believe that this book will bring hope to anyone who is walking through the valley of deep suffering.*"
--Shea Strickland, Lead Pastor, Grace Fellowship Church in Timonium, MD

"*I have known Bob and Jeanne Arnold for over thirty years. In their book, "When the Circle is Broken," they share the significant pain of losing a beautiful young daughter to a sudden and untimely death. And they share the stories of others who have also experienced the deep pain of having a child pass away. In this powerful book, we are reminded of the truth that when we confess and share our stories of pain and loss with others, we are healed.*
"*Bob's waters have always run deep, and in this book, through his journal entries, and from his time of mourning his beautiful daughter*

i

Marcie's death, he takes every reader from the deep dark waters of death and despair to the bright clear waters of hope and healing. This book and compilation of stories will be a great gift and blessing to many, for generations to come."

--Frank Kelly III, CEO, Kelly & Associates Insurance Group, Co-Founder, Fellowship of Christian Athletes (FCA), Lacrosse

"Raw. Glorious. Parents plunged into pain. Amazed by the effects of God's comfort. Grief no one would choose. Soul growth no one could regret. Who can truly sympathize with the death of a beloved daughter? The God who went through the death of a beloved Son. Jesus suffers with the suffering. Being with him transforms loss into gain, pain into wisdom, sorrow into joy. Thank you Bob & Jeanne for this gift of yourselves."

--George Miley. Founder, Antioch Network—a fellowship of apostolically-gifted leaders and the ministries they serve.

"How blessed you have been that even in the midst of your dark night of the soul, God has walked with you and spoken to you clearly bringing much wisdom and comfort. You and Jeanne will hear those words of 'Well done my good and faithful servants, enter into the joy of your Lord" AND be once again in the presence of your dear Marcie.

"Your book is so moving and truly a help to those of us that are walking a similar path. The idea of sorrow as our friend is heavy and complex. For me it is yet still sorrow and heavy to carry. So I read on with hope. Thank you, Bob, for your very dear friendship. It means so much. YOU have thrown me a life preserver!"

--Cathy MacFawn, Vice President, Allegany Coal & Land Company

"After reading When the Circle is Broken, *I was left with a sadness for one thing. —that I hadn't had the privilege of meeting Marcie Arnold. The impact she had in her 23 short years has reverberated in the lives of those who knew her.*

"Our family is a little over 3 years into the season of grief of losing our precious Brittney. We have experienced the pain that has been searing like red hot lava, to laughter, to tears, to smiles and everything in between. Through all of this I've come to realize that the God of the universe, the Savior of the world, understands my pain. In the depths of my despair, I was comforted by friends, family, and total strangers. A turning point for me was when I realized God didn't cry for me, he cried with me because he, too, felt my pain of losing Brittney. The God who created me,

created Brittney, and created the love we have for her knew better than anyone the pain of losing a child.

"When the Circle is Broken *is a book of hope. Through the Arnold's tragic loss of their beloved daughter Marcie, Bob and Jeanne lay out a path of hope and joy, all through the Gospel of Christ. God never left them, and their faithfulness manifested itself into living a full life with their family and friends. This book will help any family going through the loss of a child."*

--Doug Gorman, First District Magistrate, Warren County, Kentucky

"Over ten years ago, Bob and Jeanne Arnold got the phone call that every parent dreads the most. Their young, vibrant daughter had died suddenly from an unknown heart condition. Now, they have invited us into their most personal journey of healing and learning to live in their new reality. With years of perspective, what they offer is breathtaking. It will bring you tears and great hope. Many who have experienced pain such as this emerge from it bitter and angry, or closed off from the world and from God, afraid to ever trust again. Bob and Jeanne brought their real pain to the Lord and grew deeper into their experience of his rich love for them. God filled their dark nights with his presence. This is not a book with platitudes. This is a real journey of spiritual depth borne of brokenness. Some say that time heals all wounds, but I am not sure that's true. Some wounds never heal this side of heaven. But Bob and Jeanne share deeply about how they have come to know the real presence of Jesus even more deeply as they have brought those wounds—and questions—to him. If you take this journey, you will never be the same."

--Danny O'Brien, Founder Avila Home Care

"Anyone with a personal schooling in grief, or deeply hurting over the loss of a relationship, will find in this lament book ways to rise to new life from the grave of grief. With understated eloquence and authority, the authors open up their medicine cabinet and pass on wisdom in how to stop picking at the scabs of regret and sorrow and claim God's promises of healing and hope."

--Leonard Sweet, best-selling author of *Rings of Fire*, professor, and publisher (The Salish Sea Press, preachthestory.com)

When the Circle is Broken

Bob and Jeanne Arnold

FaithHappenings Publishers

Centennial, Colorado

Printed in the United States of America.

Scripture quotations are from New International Version, 2011. The Zondervan Corporation, a division of Harper Collins Publishers. Used by permission.

For bulk orders, please contact the author at:

Bob@meadow4.org

FaithHappenings Publishing
A division of WordServe Literary
7500 E. Arapahoe Rd. Suite 285
Centennial, CO 80112
admin@wordserveliterary.com
303.471.6675

Cover Design: Arrowdesigns

Interior Book Design: Greg Johnson

Bob Arnold (1950)

ISBN: 978-1-941555-48-4

Also available on ebook through Amazon Kindle

This book is dedicated to our beloved daughter, Marcie. She is a beautiful part of our family who shined brightly on this earth for 23 amazing years.

Marcie Renee Arnold
1979 - 2002
We will always love and remember you, until we meet again.

TABLE OF CONTENTS

Part III - Letting Sorrow Become Your Friend

Part IV - Ways of The Heart - Paths to Peace and Freedom

Part V - A Call to The Future

Author's Preface

When my daughter Marcie died in 2002, my wife Jeanne and I felt a desperation we had never felt. My sorrow over Marcie's death overwhelmed our entire family. I could find nowhere to turn for help. I cried to God, who, at first, seemed distant and silent. I was a desperate man!

The pain was so great that I had to find some answers and comfort. I began reading every book I could find on death; especially the death of a child. The stories of others who lost children were very helpful. Out of desperation, I spent a great deal of my time getting up early to be with God and trying to figure out what had just happened. I wrote journals of my thoughts, emotions, and experiences. Over the next three years, I wrote over 1500 pages. I wrote what I felt was beneficial for me. I hoped they would help me come to a place of rest amidst my sorrow.

My heart had a great big wound. But somehow, I found that the sorrow became a great friend. In the midst of my deep sorrow, I found surprising joy!

My wife Jeanne and I, now, seventeen years later, at last can say, "We would never want to lose our daughter, but we would also never want to miss the depth of our encounter with God!"

When the Circle is Broken is the story of what we have experienced since Marcie's death. I have written this book in the hope that those who have lost a child, or another loved one will find it helpful in dealing with their grief.

The many books I read after Marcie's death were quite helpful and filled with emotion. I observed that most of those books had been written within three years after the death of a child. Not many told the story of the years that followed. One of the unique features of this book is that it recounts stories and encounters from my journals written in the early years. Then, later, it walks through the entire seventeen years after Marcie's death. Each story can be read independently of the others. They do not follow an exact order of events, but rather share our deep emotional and spiritual journey at different points along the way.

Part I, *Early Reflections of Our Journey*, is written as a comfort to those going through a similar loss. My prayer is that my meditations will be with you in those moments. In writing them, I want you to know that my wife Jeanne and I stand with you in your sorrow and offer these words as a comforting presence, if only as whispers. For now, if you need the time to just meditate over your own loss and sorrow, our hope is that these reflections would serve as examples to express your own grief and sorrow.

In Part II—*Where is God in the Midst of our Sorrow*—you will encounter our thoughts about God as they matured over the years.

In Part III, we will be talking about one of the most important principles we have learned about letting sorrow become our friend and how sorrow offers a promise to transform us.

In Part IV, you will find that learning to know the *Ways of the Heart* is vital to the healing of our wounds.

In the final section, Part V—*Recent Memories and a Call to the Future*—we share our most recent memories of Marcie and how these memories help us to be brave for our future calling to serve God and others.

The book also contains several stories written by friends and family who have experienced deep sorrow. God has led us to hear and be a part of many transforming journeys. Each story brings a perspective of both pain and comfort found only in the journey of sorrow. It is our hope that through sharing our story, and the stories of others, the God of all comfort would meet you with a surprising joy, the joy that only he can bring.

PART I
Early Reflections of Our Journey

Introduction to Part I
Early Reflections of Our Journey

We begin our journey into sorrow and joy by looking at the first, very intense years of our lives after the death of our 23-year-old daughter Marcie Renee Arnold. This was a time of great pain as well as a deep encounter with God. When I read and heard the stories that others shared about their grief, I found many of their experiences were very similar to ours, especially how others had traveled the road of such immense sorrow. At times in the journey, I still became full of tears from reading all that I had journaled.

I discovered that grief has no timeline. What I felt during the first few years after Marcie's death came in waves that would continue to crash onto the shore with no apparent rhythm. So I wrote my reflections, my stories. These stories were not written as a report, in chronological order, to record the events as they occurred. Rather they were written to express my deep emotions and meditations as I traveled the most traumatic journey of my life.

The Arnolds 2001
(from top left) Marcie, Bob Jeanne, Julie, Veronica and Robert

The Call Every Parent Fears

Last night we received the most horrible news, the dreaded phone call in the middle of the night that every parent fears. The coroner from Myrtle Beach called to tell us that our oldest daughter Marcie was dead! This one phone call changed everything. It was my worst nightmare, and I could not escape.

Awakened by the phone ringing, I noticed it was around 11:30 p.m. In another room, I heard my wife Jeanne's voice screaming, seemingly alarmed. I began wondering if the call was some kind of late-night prank. Jeanne was saying: "Who are you? Why are you saying this? Marcie is not dead."

When I came into the room, Jeanne handed me the phone. A somber male voice on the other end of the line said, "This is the coroner from Horry County in Myrtle Beach South Carolina. I am in your daughter's apartment, and we found her dead. Her friends have been calling the police for the past 24 hours, trying to report a missing person. We were told she didn't report for work today, and they knew something was wrong since she had never missed work without calling. We broke into her apartment and found her. She has been dead for a few days." Ending the call, the coroner made himself available saying, "Call me anytime." No more words were spoken, and I was left with a traumatic silence as we hung up the phone.

Silence ... Numbness ... Shock! It was so sudden and so final. No pleading or negotiating. We couldn't even hope that she might get better. We felt no sense of hope. It was a blow to the depths of my soul. How could Marcie be dead? Was it drugs? How did it happen?

Our second daughter, Julie, came upstairs, having heard the commotion. Julie was the closest to Marcie of all of us. We recounted what we had just heard. Then Julie began to sob and scream, "No, not Marcie!"

What could we do in the middle of the night? All that was left was the cold, lonely emptiness of learning of the death of our beautiful, bright, young daughter, Marcie. We were trapped in a long, lonely night where death held all the cards!

We were eight hours from Myrtle Beach and had no contacts or phone numbers of any of her friends. We had no way to find out what happened. What were Marcie's last days like? How was she suddenly dead? The moments seemed as if time had stopped, and it felt cold, hard, and empty beyond belief. Surely, this nightmare couldn't be true.

The pain was so bad that I had to get away. Ten years ago, when I had heard that my brother had died suddenly, I remembered that I had gone for a walk by myself. So, I left the house to walk out my thoughts. The night sky held a full moon and a star, bright and shining, next to it. I knew God was telling me that the shining star represented Marcie, and I felt some comfort from the star's closeness.

Still, the pain and shock were so deep, so heartbreaking. I had no way to escape its terror. Why did this have to happen in the dark loneliness of night, with no one to talk to, no one to call, and no way to find out what had happened? We could do nothing but wait for answers. I could only walk a short distance before I succumbed to my grief.

When I headed home, I started to realize that we had so much to take care of. I knew the other children had to be told. Our youngest daughter, Veronica ("Vee"), was spending the night at a friend's house, so we decided to wait until the morning to tell her. Our son, Robert, was six hours away at college. We called and told him the horrible news. It was sadly frustrating because we had no way to be with him nor he with us, no way to be together in the chaotic darkness.

When we told Robert the horrible news, his lacrosse friends were at his house. They rose to the occasion and immediately called us back and offered, "Let us know what we need to do. We will do anything." They closely wrapped their circle of friendship around Robert. That night, when Robert went to bed, he began looking at some pictures of Marcie. He told us that when he closed his eyes, he saw her just as he remembered her. Robert felt close to her in that moment, and he felt that Marcie was telling him that she loved him. In his tears he spoke to her saying. "I love you too, Marcie!" He often has said that when he thinks of Marcie, he closes his eyes, and she tells him that she loves him.

At this time of night, who else could I call, and what would I say? I just couldn't call and disturb anyone. How do you tell someone that your daughter has just died? Who could I call and really count on at this moment? The pain was too great to let anyone in.

Fortunately, it was different for Julie. She immediately called her best friend since birth, Lindsay Huber, whose parents, Gary and Laura, had been our friends for over 25 years. Within a short time, Lindsay, along with her father Gary, and our good friend, Jim Gorman, arrived at our home. Years earlier, Jim had also come to our house shortly after hearing about my brother's death.

No one could say or do anything. We all quietly knew that. What had happened was far too catastrophic to trivialize. No quick fixes would be helpful, such as the fact that God had everything under control or that Marcie was now with Jesus. We all sensed that nothing could fill the void that now disturbed our souls. our friends knew they could provide no offer of hope that would console my heart. Jim and Gary also realized I didn't want to hear anything about God at that moment. They just sat with me in the paralyzing silence as I began to fathom what had just occurred. Everything was so overwhelming, and the finality of death was crushing. For what felt like hours, we just sat. Every once in a while, someone would try to say something, but it was futile. The agony was devastating and was compounded hourly by Jeanne's and Julie's pain.

How was this possible? Was this a bad dream that would be over in the morning? Our lives had now changed forever. How were we to manage the hours, days, weeks, and years ahead?

Julie and Marcie

by Julie Arnold Erb

I was there the night my parents got the call. It was the night after my senior year homecoming dance. I heard strange noises from upstairs. I went to my parents. One look at them and I knew something terrible had happened. They told me that Marcie died. "Terrible" can't begin to describe what I felt. It was the deepest pain and shock I have ever experienced. Marcie's death has shaped my life in almost every way. I think of my life in two parts: before Marcie died and after. Experiencing the loss of my sister when I was 17 divided my childhood from my adult life.

Marcie was my best friend and the person I looked up to the most. I spent my childhood trying so hard to get her approval and to never be an annoying kid sister. Marcie was always kind, and she shared her life with me. She was the best sister. I knew that all of my friends were jealous that I had her for a sister.

On my 16th birthday, a bouquet of flowers and balloons were delivered to me during lunch. They were from Marcie, who was away at college. One of my favorite memories is falling asleep downstairs where Marcie's room was in our house and being awakened by her. It was very late, and she had just come home from a concert. She was wearing bell bottoms and a halter top. As she told me all about the concert, I remember being amazed. I pictured her at Woodstock dancing with her hippie style and long beautiful hair. Marcie was so cool, and I idolized her.

When Marcie died, I felt lost, because I had spent my whole life trying to be like her. But who was I going to be like now? She died at 23; and even though I am now 35, I still think of her as my big sister.

Not only was I there when my parents got the call, I was there for the entire year of grieving with my parents. It was difficult to see them in so much pain, especially my mother. I withdrew from my social life and dove into mourning. I spent a lot of that year by myself: journaling, praying, and being cared for by my parents' amazing community of friends. I have never felt God's love more than the year after Marcie's death.

Marcie died suddenly, peacefully on her couch. We didn't know for the longest time what had happened. Even finding out about her heart condition didn't answer the question; Why? It will never make sense. What I can accept, and believe, is that God wanted Marcie with him.

Dying at 23, Marcie was spared the 9 a.m. to 5 p.m. life of paying bills, cleaning, and acquiring things. I remember feeling thankful to God that I had no guilt or remorse concerning Marcie and expressed this in my eulogy. Yes, I would have loved to see her again, but I had nothing that I needed to say to her. Our sisterhood was strong, with no regrets or wounds that needed to be healed. I knew Marcie loved me in a very special way and was proud of me. And she knew that I put her on a pedestal, above everyone else.

A year after Marcie died, I went to college. It felt like a fresh start, and I began experiencing joy again. My cousin, Lisa, died almost a year to the day that Marcie died. It brought back the full pain of loss, but the recovery was quick and less painful.

Just days after the second anniversary of Marcie's death, one of my closest friends, Jen, suffered a great loss. Her twin brother died suddenly at the age of 19. Needless to say, September is my least favorite month. I felt absolutely devastated for Jen, and for myself all over again. My loss of Marcie allowed me to care for Jen like no one else could. Throughout college, we continuously shared in our sorrow. Our friendship continues to be one of my most valued and meaningful friendships. God comforted me so I could comfort others.

God Is Sufficient for the Moment

My father died when I was 18 years old. From then on, I feared the day I would have to face the death of my mother. The prospect of being left alone evokes great fear. When my mother died 22 years later, God's grace was sufficient for the pain of the moment. In my life, God has been and is sufficient for the moment. I have always had what I needed: "The Lord is my shepherd; I shall not want" (Psalm.23:1, KJV).

Sad to say, but when my mother died, I was a few paychecks behind and didn't have enough money in the bank to go to the funeral. I thought this might have been a little unfair since I had spent my life serving God. Then, at the moment of one of my greatest needs, I couldn't even afford to go to my mother's funeral.

But God provided for that moment above and beyond what I could have imagined. I was able to attend my mother's funeral. And when the funeral was over, I had more money in the bank than ever, and it stayed that way for a few years.

The morning after Marcie died, we had to face the grim news of funeral and other related expenses. Marcie's body was in Myrtle Beach, so returning it from seven hours away would be costly. When we sat down to discuss expenses with Jeanne's sister-in-law, who is in the funeral business, we learned that the costs were way beyond anything we could imagine, let alone afford—potentially $10,000 to $15,000. The financial burden of a funeral made me feel even more helpless.

Life, being as it was, my total cash reserves in savings and checking were $78.84!

Believe it or not, I was not concerned. Somehow, I knew things would work out, and I had a sense of peace. Marcie's Marcie was so devastating that all else paled in comparison. I felt hopeless but also knew from years of watching God work that somehow it would all work out. Never in my wildest dreams would I have imagined what God arranged in the next few hours, let alone the next few days. My tears of sorrow would end up matched with tears of joy as I watched God move through the people who loved us.

Shortly after discussing the funeral expenses, one of the board members of Youth for Christ (YFC), having spoken with our friends, told me, "Plan for whatever level of funeral you need. We will pay for whatever it will cost!" He was crying, and I could barely talk. I was too overwhelmed. I was so relieved and simply amazed at how God could act so quickly. And this was only the beginning!

On Friday night, before receiving the news about Marcie's death, we went out to dinner with some friends, Jim and Bev Gorman. Eventually, Mike and Kearny, friends of the Gorman's, joined us. For years, I had been acquainted with Mike and his wife, but we had little contact. During dinner, we had a great time talking and had planned to play golf sometime in the future.

On Sunday, we received news that Kearny was going to raise $20,000 to help us pay for all of the costs associated with Marcie's death and funeral. We were again amazed. Even now, two years later, I cry when I think about it. Because of their abundant generosity, we didn't have to walk through the coming days worrying about money. So many matters would be costly: the trip to Myrtle Beach, the funeral and its large expenses, the cemetery, the meal after the funeral, Marcie's college bills, and so on. As usual, after a death, bills would need to be paid. We now had enough money to honor Marcie's life.

Through this woman, as well as the many other sacrificial ways that people gave, we wandered through the funeral, not as paupers, but as children of the King. We no longer had the additional burden of worrying about the finances of transporting Marcie's body back from

Myrtle Beach or the many other expenses. Since God had extravagantly provided for us, his children, we were able to focus on the deep pain we were facing.

When we were in Myrtle Beach, several days after the funeral, picking up Marcie's things, I remember realizing how God had provided his abundant comfort and feeling grateful for how he fortified us to walk through our time of grief. Thank you, Lord. Thank you, Kearney. Thanks to our many friends who showed us so much love by stepping up to sacrificially give in our time of burdensome grieving!

I Must Know Her Eternal Destiny

Oh, Lord, grant me the knowledge that she is with you. Right now, this is the only thought that matters. I must know that she is with you. But how can I know? How can I have the kind of assurance that I need in the depths of pain that I am feeling. Somehow, I must know, and I must know now!

My hope is that she is with you, and her grandmothers, uncles, and other relatives who preceded her to heaven. I pray she is living in a place of peace and joy beyond anything she could have ever imagined!

I am now living in the book of *Psalms*. I am surviving on its words of comfort, its wisdom, and God's presence in them. Each day God is intimately speaking, comforting me. He is meeting me in each desperate moment that I face. His words of comfort mirror the pain I feel. Amidst my great concern about Marcie's eternal destiny, I read Psalm 130 today. Listen how closely God responds to the cry of my heart:

The name Bobby is not in the Bible, neither is Marcie. I took the liberty to update verse 8 from its Old Testament context. These words were speaking directly to me.

Out of the depths, I cry to you, O Lord;
Lord hear my voice.
Let your ears be attentive to my cry for mercy.

If you, Lord, kept a record of sins,
Lord, who could stand?
But with you there is forgiveness,
so that we can, with reverence, serve you.
I wait for the Lord, my whole being waits,
and in his word, I put my hope.
I wait for the Lord
more than watchmen wait for the morning,
more than watchmen wait for the morning,

[Bobby], put your hope in the Lord,
for with the Lord is unfailing love
and with him is full redemption.

He himself will redeem [Marcie] from all her sins.

The Lord is compassionate and gracious, slow to anger, abounding in love. He will not always accuse, nor will he harbor his anger forever; he does not treat us as our sins deserve or repay us according to our iniquities. For as high as the heavens are above the earth, so great is his love for those who fear him; as far as the east is from the west, so far has he removed our transgressions from us.

Those who sow with tears, will reap with songs of joy. Those who go out weeping, carrying seed to sow, will return with songs of joy, carrying sheaves with them (Psalm 126: 5–6).

"Will the Lord reject forever? Will he never show his face again? Has his unfailing love vanished forever? Has his promise failed for all time? Has God forgotten to be merciful? Has he in anger withheld his compassion?

Restore our fortunes, LORD, like streams in the Negev. Those who sow with tears will reap with songs of joy. Those who go out weeping, carrying seed to sow, will return with songs of joy, carrying sheaves with them (Psalm. 126:4–6).

In life's great struggles, especially now in the death of a child, only the firm foundation of truth can provide a real basis for peace. Good theology leads us to deeper, sound knowledge, which affirms the depths of God's unconditional love and his total forgiveness. In this tremendous struggle and concern about knowing Marcie's eternal destiny, I can only rely on the very foundations of my faith.

Psalm 103:8–12 proclaims God's love and forgiveness:

The Lord is compassionate and gracious, slow to anger, abounding in love. He will not always accuse, nor will He harbor his anger forever; he does not treat us as our sins deserve or repay us according to our iniquities. For as high as the heavens are above the earth,

> *so great is his love for those who fear him;*
> *as far as the east is from the west,*
> *so far has he removed our transgressions from us.*

All of us have sinned, and continue to sin, to the extent that we are disqualified from salvation. I know Marcie was a sinner. I know I, too, am a sinner. If God keeps a record of sins, who could stand? Not one of us. If being good enough were the basis for getting into heaven, Marcie would have been disqualified.

But God in his great mercy, because of the sacrificial death of his Son, offers the gift of total and unconditional forgiveness. It is free to all who accept it. "Everyone who calls on the name of the Lord will be saved (Romans 10:13)! I know that very early in life, Marcie took this stand. And she shared it with her middle school friends, many whom, now, have this saving knowledge of Jesus Christ. She struggled in her classes because of it, when perhaps she was the only one who believed in her Savior and spoke up for him. Most importantly, Marcie was a person of love, one who was committed to living for Christ.

Marcie was an authentic person. In one of our last conversations riding home from lunch, I asked her about her relationship with Christ. She was firmly committed, but she shared that the arrogance of religious people in churches really bothered her. She could not relate to them.

I explained that I had spent my life trying to show people the real Jesus. I talked about how Jesus had spent most of his ministry fighting against the religious establishment, and, as a result, those people were deeply involved in the plot to kill him. I told Marcie not to allow them to be the ones who shape people's image of Christ. Most importantly, she should not let them keep her from knowing the love of Christ. My challenge was to be Christ-like and be a person that shapes her generation.

So, in the days ahead, time and again, God comforted me with an assurance that Marcie was dancing joyfully in his presence. Despite the great tragedy that I was facing, God would do great things in the lives of all of us who knew Marcie. He would use her story to draw us closer to him, way beyond what we could have thought or imagined. But for now, God has helped me to be fully confident in knowing that Marcie is with him, her heavenly Father!

What to Do with Marcie's Body?

I felt great tension about the handling of Marcie's body. It had been 24 hours since we had received the news of Marcie's death, and her body was still in Myrtle Beach. The coroner kept telling us that we had to do something with the body, as it was starting to decay. What could we do? Of course, we never had any experience with this to know what to do. Graciously, two of our friends volunteered, one having had experience in driving a hearse, to drive to Myrtle Beach and pick up her body, if needed.

I also felt great anxiety about seeing Marcie's broken body. At the time, I wasn't able to let this get to the surface of my thoughts because I did not have the courage to face reality. I, now, realize I had a tremendous fear of what I might feel when I saw the dead body of my beautiful daughter.

Jeanne experienced an even deeper anxiety. She was in a state of shock, waiting to see what would happen with Marcie's body. She had been very angry with God about Marcie's death. We decided to have her body cremated. We were on hold while we waited to receive her ashes. As I remember, we thought we would get the ashes on Monday, but they were not delivered until Tuesday. When they finally came, another crisis happened beyond anything we would have expected.

We live on a private road, and a mailman delivered the ashes directly to our home. Interestingly, he had been a friend of Marcie's when he had lived in Myrtle Beach. As he handed the package of ashes to Jeanne, what happened was unbelievable. The package that Marcie's ashes were in was leaking. How could this be? I was overwhelmed, crying, and in a state of shock! Here is Jeanne's story of what happened.

Marcie was cremated on September 30th at 7 a.m. I was devastated because I had not been able to see her body, nor have that moment to touch her. I thought of the night during the blizzard of '79 when she was born. I should have been with her when she died, or at least touched her one more time. I have had numerous nightmares after her death, and I believe it was because I did not get the closure I needed. All I had were her ashes, which came via the United Postal Service on Oct 1, 2002. I parked myself on the front porch at 9 a.m. Marcie's ashes were delivered around noon. How relieved I was that her ashes arrived. I fell apart in the front yard as bits of her ashes were spilling out of the small box.

I took the ashes and went out on our back porch and just sat with God. While dealing with my shock, I responded in anger. I remember praying, "God, show me or tell me why this happened or else I am done! I will never be able to trust you or believe in you again."

As I sat on the porch, God's comfort came to me. I opened the Bible to this verse:

"In a little while you will see me no more, and then after a little while, you will see me[.] Very truly I tell you, you will weep and mourn while the world rejoices. You will grieve, but your grief will turn to joy. A woman giving birth to a child has pain because her time has come; but when her baby is born, she forgets the anguish because of her joy that a child is born into the world. So, with you now is your time of grief, but I will see you again and you will rejoice, and no one will take away your joy" (John. 16:19b–22).

I felt an incredible, personal encounter with God, despite the horror of that moment. When I die, I will see God, and I will see Marcie. What a comfort. When God met me, I was able to be at peace with all that had just happened. God is a great Father in times of trouble!

The Amazing Night at the Funeral Home

It is better to go to a house of mourning than to go to a house of feasting,
for death is the destiny of everyone; the living should take this to heart.
Frustration is better than laughter because a sad face is good for the heart.
The heart of the wise is in the house of mourning (Ecclesiastes 7:2–4a).

For the first time since the funeral, I picked up the photo album that our friend, Edie Bernier, had put together from the pictures she had taken of the night at the funeral home. It was an absolutely amazing night, if that is possible when your daughter dies. To see the pictures of everyone is to remember the great love that people expressed that night.

Edie is one of our most faithful friends. She remembers everyone's birthday and always sends a card. Edie was a student in our Campus Life ministry back in the 70s and has been involved on different levels since then. She owns a public relations firm and does public relations for our major Youth for Christ events. Edie and I always say, as far as getting publicity, "If God has something he wants to say, it becomes a no-news day elsewhere."

When Marcie died, God had something to say, and it was a no-news day elsewhere. The news spread like wildfire throughout the Christian community in Baltimore. I am not sure how they might have heard. On Sunday, we were very surprised to hear of the number of churches that were praying for our family.

Edie did a tremendous job of getting the word out through her PR connections. Almost a full-page article about Marcie with her picture appeared in *The Baltimore Sun*. Articles were also published in the *Cumberland Times-News*, the Myrtle Beach newspaper, and our local *Parkville Reporter*. To my surprise, our local Christian radio station, WRBS, broadcast a story on Marcie's death. I thought about how many young people die every year, and outside of their obituary, so little is said about the tragedy of each death. For some reason, God had something to say through Marcie's death; so the word went out.

We arranged the usual funeral viewing hours. During the earlier viewing, a large crowd came to share in our sorrow. And when we returned, just five minutes late, for the later viewing, we were amazed. First, we couldn't find a place to park. Then, by the time we got inside the funeral home, no room was left to stand. The size of the crowd was absolutely overwhelming. For 2 1/2 hours, Jeanne and I were swamped with lines of people waiting to express their sympathy. I have never felt so loved in all my life. Believe me, as awkward as going to a viewing or a funeral feels, and finding difficulty in knowing what to say, a person's presence speaks powerfully to those in mourning! Your presence brings infinite value and tremendous comfort.

After the funeral, we learned that the traffic jam was so bad that that the police had been brought to control the traffic. People were calling their friends to tell them not to come because of the congestion, since they would not be able to get in. Some people had to park far from the funeral home and walk several blocks.

That night, God brought all of our worlds together. Having worked for 30 years in Youth for Christ (YFC), in attendance were YFC's local staff, staff from across the country, students, volunteers, fellow youth pastors, board members, donors, and friends. One of my great friends in YFC, Jack Crabtree, and his wife, Becky, came from Long Island and stayed the entire time. Jack and I went to Wheaton College together to work on our master's degrees. During that time, their children and ours became friends. Marcie and Robert learned how to swim by trying to keep up with the Crabtree boys. They were a constant, faithful presence in our lives, one that I deeply appreciated and will never forget. Their presence was a true companionship of Christian brothers and sisters.

Also with us was our large family who had travelled from New York, Virginia, Alabama, and Florida. It was the first time that all of our family was together in Baltimore.

Because for many years I had coached soccer, wrestling, basketball, lacrosse, and baseball, the people I knew from all those worlds came. They told me they were praying for me; people who I had never known from a spiritual standpoint.

Our children had attended many schools: Pine Grove Elementary and Middle, McDonogh, Boys Latin, and Maryvale Prep. Headmasters, headmistresses, coaches, teachers, and numerous students came from each school. So many people attended the viewing that we, and the place, were overwhelmed. But everyone was deeply appreciated, each one representing part of the wall of comfort that God provided.

The Maryvale community, where our daughters Vee and Julie were students, came out in full force bringing a bus load of students to the funeral the next day. Throughout the next year, they thoughtfully included a remembrance of Marcie in all their major liturgies. A few years later, at Julie's graduation, we were blessed when a special memory of Marcie was included in the ceremony. Marcie would have been at her sister's graduation and would have been so excited for her. Whenever Marcie's name was mentioned, we felt a sense that she was present. Over and over, the headmistress, teachers, coaches, and students of the Maryvale community expressed their support for our family.

We received phone calls from people all over the United States and the world. In fact, so many people called that our battery-operated phone stopped working. In the next week, we received over 600 cards in the mail and numerous emails. I printed out pages and pages of emails.

I continue looking through the photo album of the night of the funeral, now over two years since Marcie's death. I am crying the deepest tears I have cried for months: tears of sorrow for Marcie, of course, but, truthfully, I think they are mainly tears of joy for the great love that so many people conveyed by their presence that night. Every time I ride past the funeral home, I feel the deep love that was expressed that night.

The words in Ecclesiastes 7:2 have great wisdom: "It is better to go to a house of sorrow than to go to a house of feasting." You will find no more important place to express your love and support. Certainly, your presence will be good for those whom you are comforting but being there will be good for your soul as well; perhaps it is the best place for you to be.

Marcie Renee Arnold—Her Eulogy

by Beverly Gorman
Words from God to the Arnolds—October 3, 2002

To Marcie's dear sweet family, I write these words to you to strengthen your faith in your time of deepest sorrow, so that you might be sure of what you hope for and certain of what you do not see.

Marcie is my beloved daughter in whom I am well pleased. I have called her and loved her from before the foundations of the earth. Marcie has always been my joy and delight.

As I knitted her together in your womb Jeanne, my eyes saw her unformed body, and I created her to be just as I pleased. I gave her long black hair for you to play with, her soft brown eyes for you to be comforted with, and her beautiful smile for all who knew her to delight in.

I gave Marcie a strong-willed spirit, so that others might draw strength from her; while you taught her to think for herself and to be an independent woman.

I gave her an immense love for others, while you taught her what it means to give your lives to others sacrificially.

I gave her the gift of hospitality to bless others, while you showed her how to be a blessing, as you opened up your home to nourish all that needed a place of refuge and rest.

I gave her a merciful heart to counsel and encourage others, while you taught her what it means to love the hurting and downtrodden in this world.

I gave her a beautiful, joyful spirit to bring happiness to all those around her, while you nurtured her in a home that was continually filled with laughter, fun, and joy.

I gave her deep compassion for those around her, who others might disregard, while you taught her to minister to all those in pain and need.

I gave her an intelligent, logical mind with which to think that you nourished as you read to her and educated her, discussing and teaching her the key issues of life.

I gave her style and an artistic personality to draw others to me as you encouraged her to express who she was, in whatever way she chose to be.

Marcie is exactly who I knew she would be because she allowed me to mold and shape her life for my eternal purpose. I have loved Marcie with an everlasting love, and I have drawn her to me with loving-kindness. Do not be overwhelmed with the thought that she died alone, for I commanded thousands of my angels who were right there ministering to her the very second she drew her last breath. Yes, my dear Bob and Jeanne, she did not even taste death. For my Son, her beloved Savior, ushered her into my glory, where no eye has seen, no ear has heard, no mind conceived what I had prepared for my beloved Marcie.

Do not be dismayed, for there will be dark days ahead for you, but trust in the promise that I fulfilled in Marcie's life every day—I will never, never fail you, nor forsake you. You see only through a veil, a shadow of things to come, but just as you prayed, Marcie is now living in the complete fullness of my love.

I have ransomed Marcie from the power of the grave; I have redeemed her from death; "Where, O death, is thy victory; Where, O death, is thy sting?" Know this my family- that Marcie Renee Arnold is fully alive with me now, and the good work that I began in her has been completed. My sweet daughter Marcie has been received into my loving arms, her tender and faithful Father, and she is dancing with me now. And yes, you will see her soon.

One of our favorite photographs of Marcie that we displayed at her funeral.

A Letter from My Sister, Marcie

by Julie Arnold Erb

When I spoke at Marcie's funeral, I first read a very special letter that Marcie wrote to me before she went away to Coastal Carolina for college. The second part was how I felt about my sister and how much I love her. I will never forget Marcie and the beauty, friendship, love, and encouragement she brought into my life.

A letter from Marcie:

Dear Julie,

I am writing this letter to thank you for all the help you have given me in preparing to leave for school. You have done a lot for me in the last week with helping me pack and just being kind. This wasn't an easy decision, and, of course, I will never be sure if it was the right one. I guess I am a little bit nervous, but that's not all ... It makes me very sad to think you will be going to high school, and I won't be there. You are going to have a great time, and I know you will be glad you went to Maryvale.

Julie, you are a great person, sister, and friend. I just want you to know that I want you to continue to become better and better. Please be careful; don't be scared to do the right thing. There is nothing to be ashamed of in doing the right thing. This is sort of a funny letter to write; it's like a goodbye and thank you card. I guess I am sad to leave even if it's not for too long. I know you will do a good job as the oldest; and if you mess up, no big deal because everyone knows I have. I love you.

Love Always, Marcie

Words I shared at Marcie's funeral:

I love Marcie so much. I have always looked up to her. She was so beautiful, kind and the smartest person I knew. I wanted to be so much like her. I have never in my life met a person as sincere as Marcie. She will always have an effect on me. I would have done anything for her, and I know she would have done anything for me. I don't know what I am going to do without her, but I know she is part of me. I feel like part of me died along with her. She was my best friend, and I told her everything. I will continue to tell her everything because I know she is in heaven. When I close my eyes, I see her, and I know she is listening. I don't know what I am going to do without her, but I know she would want me to be happy and live the way I want to, just the way she did. I love you Marcie. I couldn't have asked for a better big sister. Never let me forget all the good times we had together. I love you always.

Angels Meet Marcie at Her Death

We feel so helpless when we think about the moments prior to Marcie's death. I am sure that every parent feels great guilt and despair at not being there for his or her child at this most frightening moment. To help relieve these feelings, we needed to find out as much detail as possible about Marcie's last days, especially her last few moments. Every event that we could piece together would help us to imagine what may have happened. Our conversations with her friends became very significant parts of putting together those final pieces. We found comfort in the words we heard about her last days, her final moments.

The information that we uncovered suggested Marcie's final moments went something like this. She served the lunch shift at the restaurant where she worked but left work early because business was slow. I think that because Marcie was a worrier by nature and needed to make sure her life was in the best order, the fact that she had little work but needed money to meet her bills may have been a source of concern.

We think that she went home and made a few phone calls. Around 3:30 in the afternoon, she was on the phone, setting up a meeting time with one of her friends for Friday night. Although this friend would never speak with us, we heard his story from some of Marcie's other friends. As they were deciding when to be together, Marcie seemed to become disoriented. Though the time was set when they would meet, she hadn't told him where. Then the phone went dead. All of his repeated calls after this received a busy signal. Because Marcie was using a cell phone, her friend assumed the reason for the busy signal was that her phone charge had gone dead.

What really happened at that moment? Did Marcie die alone? I imagine it must have been a terrifying moment of fear and frustration: how she probably felt helpless at death's immovable grip. That she was by herself and died alone was so difficult for me to consider.

We received very surprising words of comfort during the funeral service, something that we did not anticipate. Bev Gorman read her inspirational eulogy, *Words from God to the Arnolds*. These were the words that God had put on Bev's heart,

"Do not be overwhelmed with the thought that Marcie died alone. For I commanded thousands of my angels who were right there ministering to her the very second that I drew her last breath. Yes, my dear Bob and Jeanne, she did not even taste death; for my Son, her beloved Savior, ushered her into my glory."

In times like this, acknowledging that angels exist can be comforting. At the time, however, it was a statement that I was not comfortable with theologically, nor necessarily believed could happen. Was this just some optimistic, "pie-in-the-sky" wish, I wondered. Then shortly after the service, a friend of over 20 years, who didn't know Bev, came forward. She told us that after she heard the news of Marcie's death, she felt a great burden for Jeanne. She was especially concerned with how Jeanne felt about not being present when Marcie had died. She spent a great portion of the next 24 hours praying for us. Then, when she awoke on Sunday morning, God spoke to her very clearly. She shared what God had laid on her heart: "When Marcie died, she did not die alone. A host of angels was present when she died."

Quickly my mind went to the many Scriptures that speak about angels. I remembered the one thing angels always say, "Do not be afraid. I am a messenger of the Great God." In the Christmas story, recounted through Luke, angels told Mary, Zechariah, and Joseph not to fear. And, somehow, I remembered how angels would meet us at our death. The Bible also tells us that angels will accompany us when we die.

Surely these were the words of comfort Marcie just have heard at that very fearful moment. In one moment, Marcie was talking to her friend on the phone when she gradually became disoriented. She began losing control, and within seconds she lost earthly consciousness. In the next moment, she was surrounded by a host of angels. An angel quietly, confidently, said. "Do not be afraid. We are angels of the great God. We are here to accompany you to his throne." Marcie experienced great peace and comfort. She trusted her care and future to a glorious host of angels guided by her all-powerful and all-loving Lord. Marcie saw colors she never knew—rich, bold, and beautiful. She saw trees and plants— their rich beauty for the first time—and waterfalls, so loud and alive. All this captured her senses. She was surrounded by the greatest party of all time, filled with everything that she was always meant to be, a river of life evermore flowing in and around her.

Will I Dance for You, Jesus?

I discovered another fantastic message from God about Marcie. It was hidden in the many emails that I received the day she died.

Everyone knows I have no rhythm. When I dance, people take notice. But it is the kind of notice you don't want. When I was in college, I made it known to everyone that I was the best dancer in the State of Maryland. Everyone knew it to be absurd humor.

Marcie, on the other hand, despite having one leg that was slightly longer than the other, was a great dancer. That always puzzled me. But I remember watching her dance; her beauty and talent made her someone to take notice of on the dance floor.

In the days following Marcie's death, the song by Mercy Me, "I Can Only Imagine,"[i] became very popular. Many people said the song, reminded them of Marcie. When I heard it for the first time, I thought of the great dancer that Marcie was, and I imagined the great joy that she would have had when she danced before Jesus! Over and over, I have cried tears of joy, and still do, whenever I hear the song, especially the line, "Will I dance for you Jesus?" It always brings this fresh picture of Marcie joyfully dancing before her Savior!

In December, I started reviewing my emails from the day Marcie died, looking for special messages. Again, I was astounded at what I found. Because of our student conferences, I would regularly receive emails from bands and agents promoting their newest album or concert tour. As you may guess, on Thursday, September 26, at 11:00 a.m. on the day of Marcie's death, Mercy Me had sent an email to me promoting their new single, "I Can Only Imagine."

My singular thought was about the omniscience and control of our Father. September 26th was a day out of control, from our standpoint. But from the Father's perspective, things were totally in his control. At 11 in the morning, he sent me a quiet message; a message I didn't hear or could even imagine. Five hours later, earth time, Marcie was dancing before him!

Our Last Magical Moments

Knowing God the way that I do, I knew that he would have been quietly preparing my heart to deal with Marcie's death. In the days preceding her death, I knew God would have given me messages of assurance of what was yet to come. Nothing appeared to have been said or done until I started to look closer, examining the days before Marcie died.

In August of 2000, Marcie decided to leave Maryland and attend college out-of-state. She made the final decision to go to Coastal Carolina in Myrtle Beach, South Carolina. Within one week, Marcie and Robert would be leaving for college. Robert would be at Catawba College near Charlotte, North Carolina. Both would be over seven hours away from home, so, visit them frequently would be difficult. Somehow, I knew this might be the last week we would all be together as a family at our home. The week was rather dreadful week for me, so I was in the deep throes of depression.

Interestingly, Marcie's sendoff is what brought on the most sadness. Until that point, I had been more closely connected to Robert. I would have thought that his leaving would have been more depressing. I'm not sure why, but I sensed that Marcie would never return to be a permanent resident of our household. I surmised that the lure of the beach would keep her there.

For some reason, words from a song kept going over and over in my mind. It was an old song that I knew from the 60s, which was made popular again by Pearl Jam—"Last Kiss."[ii] It tells the story of a boy and girl in love. The young girl dies in a car accident. The words from the song, by J. Frank Wilson, continued to echo in my mind.

I felt that this song meant something in my life. Death was at Marcie's door. At the time, it was the death of her leaving, and probably never returning to live at home with us again. But I sensed that something even deeper was taking place.

That week, we had the dreadful task of driving to both of their colleges and leaving them behind. Marcie left for Myrtle Beach first. Later that week, we were to meet her with the rest of her belongings. Robert would ride with us. Then, after leaving Myrtle Beach, we would take him to Catawba.

To say the least, the trip was sad and dreadful. I just didn't want them to leave home. I loved having them around too much. I was unprepared for the next stage of my life.

I can't tell you how very empty our house felt when we returned. Deep sadness would fill my soul every time I would go into Marcie's and Robert's rooms. I am sure that many parents, whose children have left for college, have had the same experience, and can identify with the deep emptiness I felt.

We would mourn, and the mourning would be deep. The initial mourning of Marcie's death had actually begun that same September. I knew then that the past glory we had as a family, with all the great days with Marcie and Robert, was behind us. It was sad, at times unbearable. But slowly, God opened up new days, and the sadness relented somewhat.

I also remember the trip to Walt Disney World. In February prior to Marcie's death, we went to Walt Disney World as a family and had a great time together. Looking back, we clearly realize that this was a very special time. This was one of the last family times we shared. What a wonderful gift God had given us!

Later in that week, I visited a high school friend in Florida. A few years earlier, she and her husband had lost a son as a result of a trampoline accident. During our time together, I was able to gain a deeper look into the death of their son and all that surrounded it. Interestingly, since then, they have often visited *Marcie's Meadow,* our property in Western Maryland named in Marcie's honor. They have enjoyed the tranquility and beauty of the land.

For the past forty years, in July, we have had a family vacation in Holden Beach, North Carolina—a wonderful time when all of my family could be together. We would have fifty to seventy-five people spend the week close to each other. These treasured memories are what led Marcie to go to school at Coastal Carolina. Just over sixty days after our last July vacation, Marcie would die. This was the last time our extended family would be together. The time was magical and wonderful! That week we would continuously play, "We Dance Anyway" by Deanna Carter. It was clearly a cherished memory of some of our last times together. Our vacation was full of Deanna Carter's music and magical love expressed throughout our family! In my memory, I reflect on this most meaningful line in that s ng, *"You remember? We were laughing! We were so in love! So in love!"*

Of course, I remember the final time that Marcie and I talked— on Sunday evening, just a few days before the Thursday that she died. She seemed to want to talk more than she had in a long time. She was very concerned about not being able to secure a full-time job and was especially concerned about her finances. She thought she wouldn't have enough money to pay her upcoming bills. Later, I became convinced that her concern was partly the cause of her death, since qtc prolongation, the heart condition that no one knew that she had, can be brought on by stress. I wish I could have helped her, but the truth of the matter is that I had little money, only a few hundred dollars in the bank. As I look back on it, knowing what I know now, similar to other parents I would have given her the world. I even would have gone into deep debt if I had known that I could have relieved any of her stress.

When I think back to our last conversation, I asked when she was coming home? One moment she said something said penetrated to the depths of my soul. She, obviously, had been thinking quite a bit about this when she said, "I don't know when I'll be able to come home." Our conversation left me with a sense of not knowing when I would see Marcie again. As the conversation ended, Marcie said, "I love you!" Unfortunately, I didn't tell her the same and lost the opportunity to say to her, for the last time, "I love you!" Over and over, my soul has cried out to the heavens these words, "I love you, Marcie!" I feel confident that she has heard my cry and without a doubt, knows the depths of my love.

So much was happening that months would pass before I started to examine my days. I wanted to hear about what God was saying and doing, especially the day that Marcie died. Surely, a clear and comforting message would have come through to me. And they most certainly did.

For years, I have spent very significant time each morning reading, studying, and praying. In the days and months preceding Marcie's death, my journals reflect that I had been experiencing a dry time. Interestingly, a few months before Marcie died, Jeanne and I had begun an especially disciplined routine of getting up in the morning to do our quiet time. This was normal for me but not as much for Jeanne.

Ordinarily, I would read a few of the Psalms. And nearly every day, God would speak clearly to me from his Word. On the day that Marcie died, I read Psalm 126. When I first read it, nothing resonated. Then when I reread the passage, and meditated on it, what God was saying overwhelmed me. Two clear messages came through: one concerning Marcie's new life and the other speaking comfort for the days ahead of us.

I pictured Marcie entering the Kingdom. Read the words. Listen to the experience Marcie would have had at around 4:00 p.m. on that Thursday. Her whole world literally had changed. It had become Marcie's story.

> *When the Lord brought [Marcie] back [home]*
> *[She] was like [women] who dreamed.*
> *[Her] mouth was filled with laughter,*
> *[Her] tongue with songs of Joy* (Psalm 126:1–2, NIV 1984).

And then there was a message from that same Psalm that would take place sometime in the future, a message for us that would become our story.

> *Those who sow with tears,*
> *will reap with songs of joy.*
> *Those who go out weeping,*
> *warrying seed to sow,*
> *will return with songs of joy,*
> *carrying sheaves with them* (Psalm 126: 5–6).

This was not necessarily a story we wanted to have because we were mostly sowing tears and reaping pain. Hidden beneath the pain, however, lay a message of hope. Someday, we might again reap songs of joy. For now, our song was a lament of our deep grief and sorrow.

The Worst Day is Now Here

A week has passed since we heard the life-shattering news that Marcie had died. We have had very low times and some very high times. Overall, the time has been deeply intense and trying. The worst day is still ahead of us. Today we are heading to Myrtle Beach to close Marcie's apartment and bring back her belongings. Somber anxiety hangs over our heads because of this. In the midst of a big storm, and considerable trouble, we head south.

During Marcie's funeral, our niece's husband, who works in high security police work, was called to an emergency in Anne Arundel County. Later, we learned that a number of people had been killed in the past few days, and the authorities believed it was the work of a serial killer.

Every day we were hearing about innocent people being murdered. The killer I was being called "The Beltway Sniper." Each murder further deepened our grief. We felt the pain and tragic loss of each family and their close friends. An area on route I-95, on which we often travel, happened to be the focus of the investigation. This is near the scene where an unknown sniper had been indiscriminately shooting random people in parking lots and along the highway.

During this turmoil, we began driving to Myrtle Beach in two vans and towing a trailer. Shortly after getting on the road, we had some mechanical problems with the trailer. Our apprehension began to increase. We made it through Washington D.C., all the while listening to the news about *The Beltway Sniper*. When we got close to Fredericksburg, Virginia we heard of yet another murder. As the news was broadcast, we realized that the killing occurred in Fredericksburg just as we were passing through. The highways behind us were closed off. We had just missed it, and now all the news reports heightened our anxiety.

The ride to Myrtle Beach took nine hours, a long time to think about the depressing moment when we would enter Marcie's apartment. That would be enough of a trial in itself. First, we heard the news of the sniper; then, we encountered weather problems. Every fall in the Mid-Atlantic we face the constant threat of hurricanes. They run up the coast, wreaking havoc on everything in their path. As we traveled further south, down I-95, we heard of a hurricane moving up the coast. It was a mild one, yet another fear to face. As we got closer to Myrtle Beach, it actually struck, and we had to drive drove through 30-40 mph of hard driving wind and rain. The other van and trailer were pounded by the hard rain, with thunder, lighting, and a few funnel clouds in the distance.

When we finally reached Myrtle Beach, we were pretty beaten down. When we pulled into the parking lot of Marcie's apartment, the memories of Myrtle Beach with her, and all that we did together less than two months ago in Holden Beach, filled our minds. Our pain and sorrow increased to an almost unbearable burden. Somehow the shock of it all kept us from fully feeling the stress and anxiety that surrounded us.

Could we ever survive the moment? The heavy weight began to hold us back as we sat in the parking lot in front of Marcie's apartment. Just considering walking up the stairs felt distressing. Like so many choices in life, we had no option but to get out of the car and take the dreaded trip upstairs.

Surprisingly, as we entered the apartment, the moment was very peaceful. It felt as though the angels we had heard of filled the apartment with confidence and peace. If I had ever felt the prayers of my friends, it was certainly at that moment. Many of our friends had mentioned that Marcie had been surrounded by angels at her death. We felt as if those same angels were in the apartment to comfort us as we opened the door. Don't get us wrong, entering the apartment was extremely painful, but we both felt a strange confidence and comfort helping us face the moment. An overwhelming peace gave us strength to accomplish the daunting task ahead of us. Marcie's apartment was like a museum of mourning. Each sight, each smell, each room brought back memories.

The apartment was in very good order. Jeanne remembers that she first stopped and looked at everything. She noticed the beautiful family picture that hung on the wall and Marcie's beloved stuffed animals. She recognized all the belongings that she had taken from home to remind her of our family.

The couch that Marcie died on had been removed. There was no smell of death. Her chalkboard was filled with listings of upcoming engagements. Marcie had noted that she was to meet someone on this day, and her friend Noah was to visit her another day. Her bills were in one place, and her laundry was folded neatly on the kitchen table. Perhaps someone had come in and straightened up everything. The organization in the apartment spoke of a young woman who had been living a well-ordered life.

Jeanne was able to take charge of packing Marcie's belongings. She began to unpack Marcie's dresser drawers and search through her personal items. I couldn't muster the strength to go through each of her things because each item triggered too many memories and more pain. Jeanne began packing Marcie's bedroom belongings and began to cry as each item she saw became almost too much to bear. But Jeanne felt an overwhelming comfort come over her. She knew God was there and had Marcie in his arms: "He was there with me and would help me through." Jeanne came out of the room and told all of us that she had experienced his spirit. She knew God who had comforted her because she said she would have never been able to continue without his presence.

My thoughts were reeling! Are we really doing this? Did our first-born really die? How is it possible that we are in Myrtle Beach without Marcie, holding just her belongings?

Throughout the weekend, we met and talked with many of Marcie's friends. On Sunday, we planned to have another memorial service at a bar where she and her friends would hang out. Lots of her friends came. They talked about their friendship with Marcie, and then I shared a message with each of them. We had a tremendous time of being together, sharing our sadness and sorrow. It was a very heartwarming atmosphere within a very holy moment!

A Letter, Reflections, and a Thank You from Jeanne

A Letter to our friends shortly after Marcie died

The day after we buried our daughter, Marcie, her brother, Robert, who was 21, put Marcie's death into perspective for me with words he wrote in my birthday card.

His strength and acceptance have been an example to me. Robert wrote this note to us:

> *I guess the sun is still going to keep coming up every day. Marcie has touched so many people. Her funeral was amazing, and I know it touched so many more people. I am so happy to celebrate her new life, even though we can't be with her. We are all so proud of her. There are two reasons why she was the way she was is because of two reasons: You & Dad. I thank God every day for my family and friends. It just fills my life with happiness and love. You gave it all to me. I love you very much!*

Bob and I have been blessed with God's mercy, goodness, concern, grace, love, faithfulness, and generosity. Marcie not only experienced these same gifts from God during her 23 years with us; she turned then around and offered them to all those around her. We have received over 400 cards expressing condolences for our loss. In them we have been blessed to read so many stories of how Marcie touched people's lives, including our family, co-workers, classmates, teachers, and even strangers.

Thank you all for your love, support, prayers, and giving. Your love has made coping with this loss easier for us. Just like Marcie, you have taken your belief in God's mercy, goodness, concern, grace, love, and faithfulness and offered it to us.

Reflections (from Friends)

Many family, friends, and acquaintances wrote to share their thoughts and stories of Marcie:

There is not a day that goes by that I don't think and pray for you.
-- A common sentiment expressed to us by many

We have been praying for you faithfully since the loss of your daughter. Our hearts and Christian love surround you in prayer.
-- From Moms in Touch Prayer Ministry in La Vale, Maryland

I attended McDonogh with Marcie and found her to be one of those rare people that make you feel better about yourself for having known her.
-- Former classmate from McDonogh

She was a very special person. What a smile she had! What a sweet gentle spirit! I was blessed to have her as a babysitter. My daughter, Brandy, was crying last night as we looked through photos. She said, "Oh, Mommy, this is so sad for her mommy and daddy, but Marcie is in paradise!"
-- Marcie's former teacher at McDonogh

There is no greater sorrow, but there is also no greater love. Our hearts are broken as we think of your sorrow and share in it. Marcie was a gift to all who knew her!
-- Claudia, Joe, Zack, and Luke Harris

I met Marcie at a Super Bowl party. We talked for over an hour about her being in college and her life. I have never heard a young lady speak so highly of her family and her love of them. She simply beamed when she talked of home and those that she loved.
-- A husband and wife whom Marcie had met in Myrtle Beach

Please tell Julie that my sister and I cried together when I told her what Julie said about Marcie.
-- A friend of the family

Marcie has left her imprint in our Department of Foreign Languages: bright, articulate, and intellectually curious. We are saddened with the news and accompany you in your grief. Marcie was the best student I had.
-- Faculty of Foreign Language Department of Coastal Carolina University

We will continue to mourn with you and pray for you as you go through these days. To tell you we know how it feels, would be untrue. But to tell you that we love you both dearly is truth.

-- Glen and Lita Lowman

"Marcie"
Our love for her will never fade.
She was a treasure that you made
Our grief is strong and suffering long,
Lord, restore in us the dance,
That we might soar to worlds unknown
And see her sitting near your throne!
—by Dorothy Kielian

Thank You All So Much!

In the midst of great sorrow, we have been overwhelmed with the love of our many friends. Even in the depth of our grief, God has given us joy by showing us that he is abundantly sufficient to help in time of trouble. As musician David Parker said to me, "God knows how to be a Father when trouble comes."

While we have had great tears of sorrow, we have also wept immense tears of joy because of the love of God and the love each one of you has shown on our behalf. We can never thank you enough for entering into our sorrow with tears and sacrifice.

We are humbled by the hundreds of cards, Catholic mass cards, letters, gifts, flowers, phone calls, and food we received, enough to feed 100 people each day for a week. Surely, in a war, God's people know how to fight!

Marcie and Jeanne - Easter 2000

The Pietà
by Beverly Gorman

I want to tell you a story about a sculpture, the Pietà, and how intricately God has woven the agony and ecstasy of being conformed to the image of Christ in our lives through "a Reborn Anvil."

Two years ago, only weeks after Marcie had died, while we were all still in the grips of grieving over her death, my husband Jim was diagnosed with a spinal cord tumor. While Jim was under the hands of the neurosurgeon, I began reading a book by Ken Gire—*The Work of His Hands*[iii]—and immediately sensed that this was a holy encounter. This book is about the Pietà, Michelangelo's masterpiece sculpture of Mary holding the dead body of Christ on her lap. The book is based on pictures that photographer Robert Hupka took of the Pietà while it was on display at the 1964 World's Fair. Ken Gire relates how the Master Sculptor, God himself, is creating the transformational work of his hand through us as we share in the suffering of Christ.

I began to pray for my husband, and for the Arnold family, this prayer from the chapter on the *Wounds of Christ*: "Keep the hands you have allowed to strike us from shattering us, and use them, instead in shaping us." I gave Bob and Jeanne a copy of *The Work of His Hands* by Ken Gire along with a miniature replica of the statue of the Pietà; not understanding completely what it would mean to them.

Thanksgiving of that year, our Bible study group was having dinner together and celebrating God's goodness in the midst of all this tremendous pain and suffering. As we were talking that evening about Marcie's death and its impact on all our lives, God suddenly brought to Bob's mind what Marcie's name means, "a Reborn Anvil." He shared with us how Marcie was the chisel that God was using to shape and conform us all to the image of Christ, through the suffering we were partaking in her death. She and the circumstances of all our lives were the tools of refinement God was using as we allowed the cradled image of Christ to be released, wrestling with losing ourselves to pain, grief, and sorrow beyond what any of us had ever experienced. Through partaking in the agony of suffering with

Christ, we realized we were being conformed into his image in a way that was a holy privilege and would, ultimately, bring us great joy and blessing.

Jeanne shared that she saw herself as Mary holding Marcie's body. Her open hand was releasing Marcie into the perfect will of God, as she surrendered to the hand of the Almighty taking her precious daughter from her. Bob shared that he saw Marcie as Mary, holding Jesus in her lap; offering to us the opportunity to partake in his life, death, and resurrection just as she had. It was a powerful night.

Several weeks went by, and Bob and I had many discussions about the transforming power of the Pietà; How seeing the suffering face of Christ, the wounds in his side, the pierced hands and feet had such a deep impact on us. Little did Michelangelo, or Ken Gire, know their art would be the tools that God used to teach us that, "The suffering God allows us to experience, is the sharpest and finest tool he has in shaping us to his image and that his sorrow is his splendor."

During Christmas that year, Bob and Jeanne had gone to visit Marcie's grave. They noticed something that they had never seen before in all the times they had visited her grave and something that God had done for them that was unveiled at that very moment, in his perfect timing. There, right behind Marcie's grave, with its huge marble back facing them, was replica sculpture of the Pietà, looking out over the entire cemetery. It was so big that it was almost comical that none of us had seen it before. But there it was, in all of its beauty, majesty, and glory, the essence of what God had been teaching us through these last few months—that his body was given for us, his blood poured out for us, and that we can find hope and deliverance as we share in his suffering, in his sacrifice for us on the Cross.

What an unbelievable God we have, leading Marcie's grandfather, years ago, to buy that cemetery plot because he loved the statue of the Pietà so much. Then the remains of his precious, firstborn granddaughter would be buried there, to remind us all of God's infinite love and mercy for his tender children; for whom he gave his life.

Engraved on the top of Marcie's grave are these adapted words from the Gospel of John, given to Jeanne the day after

Marcie died: "You will see me again and our hearts will rejoice" (John 16:22). Beside those words is engraved a little smiley face, reminding us, once again, that "suffering may have a voice in our life, but it does not have the final word; the last word belongs to God." Marcie Renee Arnold: A Reborn Anvil, "Now is your time of grief, but I will see you again and you will rejoice, and no one will take away your joy."

How I know Beverly

Beverly (Bev), and her husband Jim, are two of our closest friends. We have traveled many of life's journeys together. They have been amazing supporters of my work in ministry. Jim was a longtime Chairman of the Board for Metro-Maryland Youth for Christ. Bev is a certified Enneagram instructor and has taught classes for The Meadow. Bev is also a registered nurse and has dedicated her life to helping others; both physically and spiritually.

The First Christmas Without Marcie

The first Christmas was very painful. Marcie's visit home for Christmas was not to be. The air seemed empty. We were coming closer and closer to feeling the real grief, which the shock of the event had kept from us. We needed desperately to be comforted in our mourning. The pain, grief, and sorrow overshadowed our lives. It was heavy and at times, unbearable.

A friend sent us this poem which we knew was a message from Marcie, through God. The words were a beautiful reminder of how glorious it must be for Marcie to be with Jesus and that God's love had never left us. He was there to comfort us through this deeply sad time.

"My First Christmas in Heaven "by Wanda Bencke[iv]

I see the countless Christmas trees around the world below,
With tiny lights like heaven's stars reflecting on the snow.
The sight is so spectacular... please wipe away that tear,
For I am spending Christmas with my Jesus Christ this year.

I hear the many Christmas songs that people hold so dear,
But the sounds of music can't compare with the Christmas choir
up here.
I have no words to tell you the joy their voices bring,
For it is beyond description to hear the angels sing.

I know how much you miss me; I see the pain inside your heart,
But I am not so far away; we really aren't apart.
So be happy for me, dear ones, you know I hold you dear,
And be glad I'm spending Christmas with my Jesus Christ this
year.

I sent you each a special gift from my heavenly home above.
I sent you each a memory of my undying love.
After all, love is a gift more precious than gold,
It was always most important in the stories Jesus told.

Please love and keep each other, as my Father said to do.
For I can't count the blessings and love he has for each of you.
So have a Merry Christmas and wipe away that tear,

Remember, I am spending Christmas with my Jesus Christ this year.

A Second Death Has Occurred

The news is again, devastating! Oh, Lord, how can this be?

After Marcie died, especially because of the way she died, we were advised to have all our family members checked to see if anyone else had any kind of special heart problem. Jeanne pursued this intently, not wanting to experience another child's death. Then the devastating news came back: most of our family is predisposed to the same genetic heart condition. It is called qtc prolongation which results in arrhythmia. As best as we can tell, it is what caused Marcie's death.

After our children Marcie, Julie, and Robert's births, we decided to have another child. One of our main motivations sprang from the great joy we experienced with our first three children's involvement in sports. Most of all, I wanted another boy whom I could coach and help excel in athletics. Quite frankly, I was disappointed when we found out that we weren't going to have a boy. Despite what the doctors told us, I believed against all hope, that the baby inside of Jeanne was a boy.

Well, I was wrong! We had a beautiful little girl whom we named Veronica or "Vee" for short. Our youngest child grew up to be an accomplished athlete. The joy and the lesson from God, who gives perfect gifts, was that Vee was the perfect gift to us.

As a natural athlete, she has loved and played lacrosse since she was five years old. When she was six, she came in first place in her swim team's league championship. At 10, she made an AAU basketball team and traveled to Walt Disney World to compete in a national championship. Vee also had great success in running and playing soccer. She told me she didn't understand how other kids could live and not play sports.

Vee and I walked side by side through all these years. In many situations, I was her coach. In all situations, I was her mentor and greatest encourager. We developed a very close relationship during these activities. When I coached, and especially when I coached Vee, I felt close to what I was created to do.

For Vee's young adult years, lacrosse had been our primary love. I helped coach her lacrosse team and stood in for the head coach when he was on vacation. We participated in two tournaments and were delighted that we won both championships.

We had developed many close friendships with the girls on our team and their parents. We were weeks away from Vee's next lacrosse season when our family was going through the medical testing precipitated by Marcie's early death.

I loved coaching Vee and her friends and to be with their parents anticipating a great season. But then we received the distressing news. We were told that Veronica should never, again, play sports of any kind. The genetic heart condition that runs in our family prohibits us from playing sports. For Vee, Julie, and Robert, athletics of any kind, could possibly lead to an arrhythmia, which could result in death.

Vee and I were devastated. How could this be? The walls of death were threatening to strangle me. Again, I had no room for negotiation: no lacrosse, no basketball, no swimming, no soccer, and no volleyball throughout the rest of her high school years. The doctor warned us that Vee shouldn't even jog.

All our hope and anticipation for the upcoming lacrosse season was destroyed. Vee's future in athletics had ended. I cried and cried. One time when I was crying, Vee very confidently told me, "I'll play lacrosse again. Don't cry Dad."

But for now, we could do nothing. We had to go by the doctor's advice. How could we take a risk and have yet another child die? This was devastating. We were in a very lonely and desperate place. Couldn't God just heal her and end all of this? No answer.

This lacrosse season was so important that we stayed on just to be a part of the team. I continued to coach, and Vee came to every practice. I was so proud of her. She was so strong, maintaining a great attitude, despite not being able to play. Well, then we experienced a miracle and a deliverance of sorts.

Everyone wanted to help. Person after person comforted us telling us they were willing to do anything they could to help us, and they did. In a few days, our friends connected us with the best doctors in Baltimore, as well as the top experts in the country who were familiar with the condition, qtc prolongation.

One expert doctor in Philadelphia gave us some hope. He informed us that Vee, possibly in six months, could play one low impact sport, maybe volleyball or something like that—but for now, none at all.

After six months, Vee was allowed to play in a few lacrosse games in which we were way ahead and with minimal risk. Gradually, Vee played in essential situations, while being disciplined not to do much running. She played a position where she could remain close to the goal.

Soon thereafter, a miraculous event occurred. We were, yet again, an excellent team and had made the finals of the league championship. The afternoon was beautiful for lacrosse, sunny and 90 degrees. The game turned out to be one we would never forget. It was very competitive. We were ahead by two; then the other team took the lead by four. With a few minutes left, we were down by one. We scored again, tying the game with just 50 seconds remaining.

We got the ball and ran to the goal. Time was running out, so we took a shot but missed. The opposing team's goalie now had the ball, but, for some strange reason, she stepped out of the goal. A goalie very rarely does in lacrosse. As she stepped out of the goal, one of our players checked her stick. Amazingly, the ball fell right into Vee's stick, and she quickly turned and took a shot. As I felt the anticipation swell, I cheered as she scored the winning goal. The clock ran out, and Vee's team won the championship!

Yes, Vee scored the goal, but God was there with her. I knew that after all the disappointments over the past months, this was not just a great sports victory but a clear sign of God's love, encouraging us to move on to face the many other hurdles we would encounter.

I Need You to Move Now

"If I only knew where to find [God]" (Job 23:3).

The events in my life have, again, spiraled out of control. I need God to move quickly and miraculously. The following passage from Frederick Buechner's great devotional, *A Room Called Remember*, is the one that God led me to read today, June 15, my birthday. It is titled, "Listening to Your Life" At this point in my life, it is a crucial message that I desperately need to know.

> *"And the promise is that, yes, on the weary feet of faith and the fragile wings of hope, we come to love him who first loved us: loved us in the wilderness, especially in the wilderness, because he has been in the wilderness with us. And we shall rise out of the wilderness. This is the greatest promise! Wait—hope—trust, believe in God's goodness in the land of the living."*

In his book, *Waking the Dead*, John Eldredge reminds us how much we underestimate the importance of spiritual warfare in our lives. He makes a remarkable statement about woundedness that has clearly defined my world since I have read it. He uses the analogy of Satan and his cohorts as sharks smelling blood. The blood rouses the shark to attack. When Satan is aware of a wound, he realizes the potential to attack and destroy a person. Our deep wounds can leave us open and vulnerable to destruction.

Between Satan, and the natural affairs of life, a deep attack has occurred on our family and friends, like multiple waves hitting the beach. Let me recount the devastation that occurred soon after Marcie's death and the months that followed.

Immediately after Marcie's funeral: Jeanne's Uncle Bill had surgery and went into a coma for a few months; our very good friend and Youth for Christ Board Chairman, Jim Gorman, was diagnosed with a growth on his spinal cord; another friend woke up to find her husband in the throes of grand mal seizures, so many that the doctors had to go to special measures to stop them. Shortly after that, our nephew attempted suicide, and another close friend's sister died of an overdose. Each week, for months, tragedies struck our family or close friends. It was the beginning of a wrecking ball that was crashing hard into the very foundations of our lives.

And that was just the beginning. In January, I was leading a weekend of spiritual renewal for our Youth for Christ staff. A lot of what I intended to speak about was the mourning process that my family and I had gone through. The week prior to the retreat, my body was racked with pain. My knee became inflamed, and I was only able to walk with a severe limp. For the first time in my life, I developed an ear infection. The right side of my face hurt so bad that I couldn't sleep. My right arm was numb as well. The whole right side of my body felt as though it was being immobilized. The pain was excruciating.

On top of that, problems with Jeanne's job began to occur. Her employer seemed to have little concern for the pain we were going through. During an interview with her boss, Jeanne was asked why her productivity was going down. It seemed like an incredibly insensitive question and one that had a fairly obvious answer. When Jeanne replied that it was because of the death of our daughter and that she was still dealing with her grief, he countered that she didn't appear to have been affected by it that much. Jeanne could tell by his attitude that she was on the verge of being fired. With everything else going on, we didn't need a severe decrease in our finances. Thus, to cope with the overwhelming pressure, Jeanne had to take medical leave and was subsequently able to receive compensation for the next few months.

As I look back on my journal at this point, I was getting in touch with the deep pain that I felt. Let me share the depths of my despair:

> *I am worn out. I am at the end of all ropes. Crushed; near the point of being knocked out. There's nothing left to fight with. I can't take anymore. I don't know how to pray. I don't know what to pray but Help!! The life I am living is so intense, so overwhelming. I don't know if I can go on any longer. I need God's hand to come and restore me emotionally, to give me more vision and new weapons of warfare. Deliver me into your strength, your vision and might!*
> *Father, is there any rest? Is there any peace?*

*I am now at a point where I don't think any man or woman
could answer the great dilemmas I am now facing. The water
continues to get deeper. There is no such thing as good news anymore.
I am desperate for you; I need to hear from you. Give me your
wisdom, your power, your comfort. I can't find you. I can do nothing.
He remains silent! Unmoved: Where is my help? The problems
mount ... my anxiety roars ... Where is God?*

And there on the coffee cup in front of me I read, 'Stop
whining and start paddling!'" Sometimes, God is so empathetic!
And in my Bible study, I turned to this verse, "Take up your
mat and walk!" *Oh, if I could find out, what he's truly up to?*

In early March, as I was reading, I had a sense that I would
be put to a major test. I thought: Am I not already in
overwhelming circumstances with Marcie's death and all its
aftermath? But then, I knew I would face more severe
challenges. At the end of the test, however, I would have tears
of joy and deliverance.

Within a short time of sensing that I was in the middle of a
major test, I was confronted with several complex and
overwhelming issues. We were given the medical diagnosis that
Jeanne, Julie, Robert, Vee, Jeanne's sister Crissy, and her
daughter, Jordan, all had qtc prolongation Syndrome. A week
later, shortly after a family wedding, my niece Lisa who was the
first cousin in a long line of grandchildren was diagnosed with
brain cancer and was given just six months to live. She was only
50 years old. Since I am the youngest in my family, I was always
closer to many of my nieces and nephews than I was to my
brothers and sisters. Lisa was one of my favorites. She was at
my house nearly every day when I was growing up. Though this
was devastating news, I was unable to feel all the impact
because I was still reeling with Vee's bad news of no longer
being able to participate in sports.

This was an extremely difficult and depressing period in my
life. And only by reading through the Psalms was I daily
reminded of God's faithfulness and deliverance. Even with that
comfort, I was totally and emotionally exhausted. This is what
I wrote in my journal in late April, about a month after this
series of blows.

I am again residing in a pit: a pit of despair, where there seems to be very little hope.

All the events of my life have led me to exhaustion with little hope or faith.

Lord, have mercy on me—a sinner. Let me see your deliverance in the land of the living right now even though there appears little hope, little purpose.

Again, I read the words in the Psalms which spoke to my despair and gave me hope. "Though you have made me see troubles, many and bitter, you will restore my life again; from the depths of the earth, you will again bring me up. You will increase my honor and comfort me once again" (Psalm 71:20–21).

But when would my deliverance come? I needed it immediately! Lacrosse season would be over in two months. Lisa only had six months to live, and most of that would be painful to go through. How will we survive without the income from Jeanne's job?

I look for, I long for, and I desperately need the miraculous movement of God in my circumstances. I know nothing is impossible for God. I cry to God to heal Vee. What am I thinking when I pray this, since I have yet to experience it? I have seen God do great things, but he seems to be withholding. I haven't seen a lot of the miracles that Christ did: the healing, the supernatural interventions, the blind see, or the lame walk. I want so much for miraculous interventions: for Vee to be healed, for Lisa to be healed, and for God to reach down and give Jeanne a new job. Yet, I wait and wait. I pray and pray, but no answer.

As I look back to that period, I can see the message was clear. I re-read what Phillip Keller wrote. It made perfect sense in our crisis. God was doing something; something not to my liking, but something supremely good. His words make perfect sense now. I read the words during the crisis but couldn't clearly hear them:

Don't rush things, don't demand instant results, but learn to wait quietly for him to set the stage and direct the drama of your days.

Oh, Master, you haven't changed. You are still the beloved Physician that can heal. But you are about far more than healing. Waiting for God is a spiritual secret in walking with him. It does not come in some stirring vision overnight. It comes softly, day by day, as we walk gently with him in his ways.

but those who hope in the LORD *will renew their strength. They will soar on wings like eagles; they will run and not grow weary. They will walk and be faint* (Isaiah 40:31).

Blessed is the one who perseveres under trial because, having stood the test, that person will receive the crown of life that the Lord has promised to those who love him (James. 1:12).

Dear friends, do not be surprised at the fiery ordeal that has come on you to test you, as though something strange were happening to you. But rejoice inasmuch as participate in the sufferings of Christ, so that you may be overjoyed when his glory is revealed (1 Peter 4:12–13).

"Abiding" means staying with Christ through the difficult times. *Heal my manipulative spirit.* God will bring the level of pain into your life that he deems necessary to conform you into his image. The same perplexing refrains keep running through my mind:

I can't find you. I can do nothing. He remains silent! Unmoved. Where is my help?

The problems mount ... my anxiety roars... Where is God? Oh, if I could find out, What he's truly up to?

A year later, I am reminded of those dark days. Looking back, I can see God's overwhelming presence surrounding me. I had no clear guidance, nor had I sensed a clear presence, especially, not then. But now, it is clear. Each day I experienced a deep abiding and knowing. God is an ever-present help in times of trouble. He is very present, but not usually in the ways we would think or would like him to be. He doesn't often rescue us in miraculous ways, at least, not right away. He is doing something far greater than we in our small minds can understand. We will discover that God is far greater than just a miracle worker.

The paradox of what I am facing and what I know about how God works is often clouded and bewildering to me. My troubles seem to be far from over, and I fear that the days ahead will bring even more sorrow. But thankfully, the blessings that are ahead will also be beyond what I can imagine.

God will deliver me and teach me lessons I will never forget. *As my life continues, I will return to the truth of his surprising joy even in the midst of my troubles.* I will never be able to thank God enough for doing exactly what he has done.

Another Late-Night Call

Ever since we received that fateful late-night phone call about Marcie, anytime the phone rings late at night, my anxiety begins to flow. I anticipate bad news from who is on the other end of the phone. Many times, it is just a wrong number. Two nights ago, the phone rang at 2:15 a.m. I could tell that it was not a wrong number because Jeanne was engaged in a conversation. Who could it be? What could it be? It can't be good.

Our daughter Vee was spending the night at her friend's house. In the middle of the night, Vee became sick and started vomiting. Of course, she wanted her mother and needed to be picked up. I became concerned that she was sick, but at least it was not another tragedy. The relief made the moment better than expected.

I had to drive 40 minutes; and when I picked Vee up, she was rather distressed. She had been crying and was embarrassed because she had thrown up on her friend's bed. Now she just wanted to be home to weather the storm. She repeatedly thanked me for picking her up. I was sort of surprised. anyhow could she doubt that I would always be there for her? Picking her up from her friend's house, seemed like just another one of those things. I would do anything I could for any of my children. But her appreciation kept being expressed: "Thank you for picking me up. You know I would do it for you if the same thing occurred. I love you Dad!"

"I love you too, Vee," came easily from my lips.

Almost immediately, that moment took me back to the opportunity I had missed when I didn't tell Marcie that I loved her the last time we had spoken on the phone. When the conversation had ended, Marcie had told me she loved me, and I remember just saying good-bye.

Why do I have such a difficult time telling my children that I love them? Nothing is more important to me than my children. For the past 25 years, they have been the greatest joy in my life. Every day, when I wake up and when I see them, they bring me rekindled joy. Each of their accomplishments has filled me with pride. Where they have struggled; I have struggled with them. Yet, I had always had trouble expressing my love for them.

This story was a defining and extraordinary moment that I will never forget. Easily and without hesitation, I confidently said, "I love you!"

PART II
God in the Midst of Sorrow

Introduction to Part II

God in the Midst of Sorrow

When we encounter the death of a loved one, we tend to question God. Where is he when we hurt so deeply? How could he allow this to happen? I thought he was good. How can we find him in the middle of our sorrow? Where is he during our pain?

Over time, we came to find that God is very present with us in our sorrow and pain. We find that death is our enemy, and it is also God's enemy. Saint John of the Cross revealed in his writings that God is not absent but very present in our pain. When we are hurting, however, we have difficulty recognizing his presence. God's deep and rich love is unfamiliar to us. But be assured that God, also known as "a man of suffering, and familiar with pain" (Isaiah 53:3), is a great friend in times of trouble.

I do not pretend to be an expert on the issues dealt with in the following chapters. Feel free to disagree with anything I say. But, when we consider what God says, he is bigger and more wonderful than any of us can think or imagine! I can only hope that at least some of what I say will help you see that God is on your side. That the sorrow you feel was first felt by God. I truly hope that you would come to know that he is with you, and that he really understands the depths of your sorrow.

Getting Personal

One never understands how some people can experience an enormous amount of pain while others have little or no pain. It's a mystery! Nancy Fallace has had far more pain in her life than the normal person.

Over the last forty years, I have reading the book of Psalms many times, and during the pandemic I have been reading it over and over. I also have been reading some outstanding books written about Psalms. The Psalms are the songs and poems written by people who, in many cases, were walking through deep pain. And they have expressed themselves with complete honesty. Open about their feelings, they have no problem questioning God about how unfair their pain is.

Honesty is key to processing pain and getting healthy. when talking with hurting people we encourage them to be honest with God. He can handle all our frustration and anger. In fact, he wants us to be honest with him in times of trouble.

Nancy is a great example who is honest about her thoughts and feelings. Total transparency can be scary but will help us integrate our pain spiritually and psychologically. Nancy is an amazing woman. She still doesn't have many of her questions answered, but her presence speaks powerfully about how her honesty has helped her process her pain.

To those who express their pain and sorrow, we can be tempted to give advice try on how to overcome their struggles. The last thing Nancy or any of us need when we're going through deep sorrow is for someone to provide easy answers. The best we can do is listen and sincerely pray for them. And if we listen closely, we will find that they, like Nancy, are walking in a deep intimacy with God.

You Have Been Through Too Much
by Nancy Fallace

I often hear, "You've been through too much in your life!" more times than I care to count. What is the appropriate response to that statement? Hearing it, has sometimes made me think that it's just the consequence of my crazy years in my youth full of making bad decisions. Other times, I am struck with the unfairness of it all and wonder why other people seem to sail through life, with their only sorrow being the death of their 95-year-old grandparent or their 15-year-old dog. But having lived with trauma and grief for more than half my life, I realize that life and death, trauma, and joy, are all a great mystery. All of us are fair game, and the only control we really have, is how we respond to all of it.

I grew up in a stable, loving Christian home surrounded by family and great friends, always feeling completely secure. All was good, up until my sophomore year of college, when my 19-month-old nephew did not survive surgery to correct a congenital heart defect. My neatly, put-together formula of what to do, how to pray, and what to believe in order to avoid tragedy was blown to bits. What about Matthew 21:22, "If you believe, you receive whatever you ask for in prayer." It would be years, before I realized that the more we concede to the mystery of it all, the more control we release, and the more room we make in our hearts for peace and gratitude.

I was married for a rough seventeen years and had three children. When my husband died, suddenly, in our home of a pulmonary embolus, our girls were 7, 8, and 14. I went back to grad school to pursue a career as a Speech Language Pathologist, and within the next few years, met and married my soul mate, Nick. In 2010, we found out that my middle daughter's complaints of blurry vision were the result of a hereditary degenerative eye disease, which will eventually take her central vision.

My world, as I knew it, ended in October of 2014. My youngest daughter, Hannah, was picked up from work by her boyfriend, Charles, and within ten minutes, they were both killed in a horrific accident with a dump truck. They were 19 and 20. I found out when a local news station posted a breaking news article on Facebook, only to have it confirmed three and a half hours later when the police showed up at my house.

If you have walked closely beside any other parent in this unfortunate club, you may have a slight glimpse of the horror, the disbelief, the feeling of going crazy, wanting to die, never ending tears, and years and years of physical and emotional anguish that follow. Losing a child is not something that you get over; it is not something you "move on" from. Hannah was a living, breathing part of me; a part of me that died.

In every way, I am a different person now. Severe emotional wounds, similar to physical injuries, may eventually heal but leave scars that change the way we operate. In those early days, I really believed I was going crazy. The reality of never seeing your child again, is simply too much to absorb. Her things were all where she left them, and her room still smelled like her. She left a half-empty water bottle there and a spoon stuck in an open container of ice cream in the freezer. On the day of the accident, she sat at the kitchen table with me making roses out of clay. Her fingerprints are still on every petal.

I never saw Hannah after the accident. It was too horrific. Nick shielded me from the horrid details by handling everything with the coroner and the funeral home. The decisions that had to be made are ones that I wish no one would ever have to make.

Night after night, Hannah never came home. The things in her room started getting dusty. Eventually, I threw away the ice cream in the freezer and the trash in her room.

Years later, I would muster the strength to touch her things, throw more away, and put her clothes and jewelry in bins. I go months, now, with no one ever mentioning her name. Most of her friends have "real" jobs at this point, and some have gotten married and moved away. A couple of her closest friends have babies, and Hannah would be an aunt, now, to Wilson. She's missing out on so much, and we wonder what her influence would have been on Wilson, knowing that even he will be different, not having her in his life. Along this path, I've met and become friends with other bereaved mothers who also lost teenagers very close in time to when Hannah left us. We gain strength from watching each other keep going, eventually, integrating joy back into our days.

I find that the grief doesn't change much. It certainly is less intense now, five years later, and I have more control over it when I allow myself to feel it. I've learned to compartmentalize my grief, partly because it becomes less, and less acceptable to openly grieve after five years. Thank God that most people just don't understand what I'm going through. But that means my grief is now mine to share strategically with my family and, sometimes, closest friends, only when the risk of making them uncomfortable is acceptable, such as on her birthday or the anniversary of the accident.

How does a grieving mother come to terms with the "good God" she has been taught about her whole life in light of the violent and sudden death of her child? Suddenly the world is not safe. Everything is an unacceptable risk. Everyone becomes a stranger. In *A Grief Observed*[vi], C.S. Lewis states, "No one ever told me that grief felt so much like fear. I am not afraid, but the sensation is like being afraid." Five years later when the days start getting shorter in the fall, every evening my body becomes afraid, like the feeling that something horrible is about to happen, or perhaps did happen, and I just don't know about it yet. I start going through my family members in my head, recounting where they are, sometimes, checking on them just to make sure.

Once something terrible happens to you, you don't expect that things will "be fine" anymore. It changes everything, and for me, it has especially changed my view of God and prayer. Growing up in the church, we tend to learn what I see as a "formula" to keep God in check: daily quiet times, regular prayer, Scripture study, socializing with like-minded friends, and regular church attendance. We pray diligently for people to be cured of cancer, to be safe in their travels, to get into the right college, or to be blessed financially.

When we perceive that those prayers have been answered, we rejoice, proclaiming that God heard our prayers and that God is certainly good. We don't hear much about the goodness of God when our prayers aren't answered. When my nephew died, I was certain that it was because I didn't pray "hard enough" with enough faith or didn't confess some sin that caused God to not hear my prayers.

Why do Christians seem to think that if we are diligently following God, our lives will go smoothly? We won't have financial hardship; we'll avoid tragedy in our families; we'll be healed from all illnesses. Where did we ever get that idea? Wasn't Jesus himself hated? He didn't have a home, and he died a horrific, painful death.

It's all a great mystery, and Father Richard Rohr says it much better than I can: "God is light, yet this full light is hidden in darkness, (John. 1:5); so only the sincere seeker finds it. It seems, we all must go into darkness to see the light, which is counter-intuitive for the ego. We resisted this language of 'descent' (*going into darkness*) and overwhelmingly made Christianity into a religion of 'ascent,' where Jesus became a self-help 'savior', instead of a profound wisdom-guide, who really transforms our minds and hearts." Rohr goes on to say in his devotion, the *Mystery of Suffering*[vii], "Many of the happiest and most authentic people I know, love a God who walks with crucified people and thus reveals and 'redeems' their plight as God's own. For them, God is not observing human suffering from a distance but is somehow *in* human suffering, *with us and for us*. Such a God includes our suffering in the co-redemption of the world, as "all creation groans in one great act of giving birth" (Roman. 8:22).

What I know is that love lives on, and God is love. I see him in every expression of love in my day-to-day encounters. It's what matters—not bickering over theology or excluding people because they don't believe the same thing as you or live in such a way that is "acceptable" to you.

Hannah's departure left us with a lot of love, with nowhere to go. I can't hug her anymore or buy her something just because. That love is God, which needs to be shared and poured out. Hannah was known for loving the outcast and taught all of us how to love unconditionally. And that is something that everyone can take from her short life.

Go and love.

How I Know Nancy

I heard of Nancy's story and invited her to share it at one of The Meadows' Mystery & the Great Sadness workshops. After meeting Nancy, and hearing her story in person, our friendship grew. We shared a similar depth in our suffering, and I knew both our hearts longed to find God in the midst of sorrow. Her story touched my soul, as it had touched so many others.

Mystery and Marcie's Death

When we began to try to figure out why Marcie died, we were left with no answers. To have a nice formula to explain it all would ae been great, but we had none. I realized that even if we had all the wisdom from all the people on earth and the most sophisticated computers, we could not answer our question. We were left only with mystery.

For most, mystery is an unsettling concept. Protestants have an obsessive, compelling need for clarity. Mystery, ambiguity, and uncertainty are the places where reason brings us to the end of ourselves—a place where we have to stop; stop and take off our shoes (see Exodus 3:5). If we don't stop, these mysteries will prove too much for us. If we must have all of our questions answered, some days when we won't be able to move forward. But we can look to the God of the universe. As we do, we find One who is powerful beyond belief, a mystery that existed before time and eternity, and a love that is beyond comprehension.

A few years ago, I spent a weekend with Hugh Ross, a Christian astronomer. Afterwards, I spent time reading his research on the universe. Remarkably, that information is now outdated because every day more, and more, is discovered about the universe.

At that time, I learned that more than 1 billion trillion (1,000,000,000,000,000,000,000) stars in the universe had been discovered and recorded. Even so, this fact was limited by what they could merely observe, and that the universe continues to expand. The staggering reality is that 99% of the cosmos still remains unseen! If we can't see or understand 99%, how can we imagine to fully understand God. He is infinitely beyond comprehension!

Psalm 139:17, God declares, "Your thoughts are far beyond my understanding; much more than I could ever imagine" (CEV).

A greater and even more amazing part of God's mystery is that He came to live among us on earth. In chapters 15 and 16 of his book, *The Impact of God: From Soundings of St. John of The Cross*,[viii] Iain Matthews writes about how God reveals himself in the person of Jesus Christ: *God is a love: unlike any that we know. God's love, its height, width, depth, and length, is beyond imagining! Christ is an unfathomable mine: with layer after layer of treasures!*

Where does that leave us in our search for answers? We come to learn to live with mystery because we are not capable of knowing all the answers. We come to live, knowing with certainty that God is love and God is strong. With his strength and love carrying us, we recognize that he, personally, suffers with us. His presence is sustaining us through our great time of sadness. To deal with the depths of my sadness, I had to return to the truth of Psalm 62:11, that *God is love, and God is strong:* "One thing God has spoken, two things I have heard: 'Power belongs to you, O God, and with you, Lord, is unfailing love.'"

After Marcie's death, the mystery of not knowing and not being able to understand kept me running back into God's arms. I continued to have faith in his strength and unfailing love. I experienced a few incidents when this was confirmed in the observable world, but mostly I had to trust in what I could not see. In many times of sorrow, we must surrender to the mystery and just find strength in God's love for us.

All Suffering Is, First, God's Suffering

In 2010, I read what Teresa of Avila shared about her experiences: "I desire to suffer, Lord, because Thou didst suffer." [ix]

Before we are aware of our suffering, God was intimately involved and suffered, first, for the losses we would experience. We are, first and foremost, his children. Just as he shed a tear for his friend Lazarus's death, he also shed a tear for our suffering. I began to realize that Marcie was, first, God's child, and that he was the first to suffer the sorrow of Marcie's death.

The profound reality is that our God also came and experienced the same pain. The symbol of our faith is a cross. Christ's suffering and death on the Cross far exceeded anything that we will suffer. He entered fully into our human experience in all that we encounter in life. He wept, mourned, and suffered with Marcie's death just as we did. We need to realize that in the midst of our sorrow and suffering, God was and is present with us.

Death is his enemy; just as death is our enemy. He conquered death in dying on the Cross and gave us new life through his resurrection. and he assures us that when we enter his suffering, we enter his glory.

Now if we are children, then we are heir— heirs of God and co-heirs with Christ, if indeed we share in his sufferings in order that we may also share in his glory.

When we have children, we take on both the joy and sorrow of parenting. We become caretakers of God's children, and in doing so we share in God's glory. Children's Television series host, Fred Rogers reminds us that when suffering occurs, we see the heroes arise[x] (*You Are Special: Neighborly Wit and Wisdom from Mister Rogers*). The Christian community stood by us in our grief and sorrow. So many mourned our tragedy and entered into our suffering. Each one helped us carry our burden and lighten the load. God's greatest glory is that he suffers with us. Often, even unaware, we enter into our greatest glory when we enter into the suffering of others.

Getting Personal

The moment we hear that our love one has died tragically or suddenly is a moment we will relive live many times over, trying to figure out what exactly happened. At that point, death holds all the cards, and we are left with very few options. We go into a state of shock, which somehow helps us to avoid the massive pain we are facing. In that moment, nothing is more important than to cling to the to God who is very present to us with his love and his mercy. Even then, he can far away and silent. Cathy found God in the midst of her crisis, and that was her only hope!

An Encounter with God
by Cathy MacFawn

When I received my husband's phone call confirming the death of our son, Breandan, from a helicopter crash, I heard in my spirit the words of Peter; "Lord, to whom shall we go? You have the words of eternal life" (John 6:68). That was God holding me in the midst of my overwhelming pain and sorrow.

The first words that Bob Arnold spoke to me were, "Cathy, what you must know and believe is that God is *still* good, God is *still* faithful, and God is *still* loving." That was God through Bob, a dear friend and one acquainted with such grief, throwing a life preserver to a faltering believer.

My sorrow became raw as I thought about life experiences never to be for Breandan: the raising of his boys to adulthood, trips and experiences never again to be shared, no more the warmth of a family embrace. And for me as a mother, the realization of the deep and scarring sorrow now forever etched in the hearts of his sister and brother.

Yet, I found that just as God can keep us in our sorrow, he does not turn away when that pain erupts into anger. And as we ask, we know his forgiveness. That is God embracing a raging child as she beats her fists against his chest chaffing at the embrace until, exhausted, she finally relaxes into to the comforting arms of her loving Father.

How I Know Cathy

Cathy was a cheerleader when I played basketball in high school. Our journey continued when we both found Christ in different areas of the country, she in Arizona and me in Baltimore.

The Intimacy of Pain

As the months passed, I began to reflect on what Marcie's life must be like now. One morning, during my time of silence and meditation, I saw an image of her life more vividly. I saw Marcie on a shore, looking back and smiling, longing for the day when we will meet her again. Marcie's life was now completely in God's hands. She knew we were in his care. She knew God as all love. She knew that he has our future. She knew what we will face and see when we get to heaven. And his love will conquer and comfort our fears, doubts, guilt, and questions. Marcie is not lonely for us, nor does she fear our future.

Marcie's death does not bring questions about God's goodness. Sure, I could think, Why? After all, I am a pretty good person, a youth minister for over 30 years. Why would God have brought such misfortune into my life? Certainly, I didn't deserve the fate that life has brought my way.

I can't hold on to Marcie. I feel as if I own nothing in life. I am a poor casualty who only owns the grace and mercy of God as he meets me in every situation. Somehow here is where I have come to know that God is loving and great. My acceptance is the only way home.

What I know in this present moment is that Marcie knows even better because she is in God's presence. If the Lord had not been on our side, wow! Where would we be? For those of us who live in deep pain, we can easily feel as though God is punishing us or that he has abandoned us. Yet just the opposite is true. God is present in our pain. He is not there as a rescuer to take away all our pain. I waited for that to happen, of course, hoping that would be how God would comfort me. But the pain remained and intensified.

God gave us his Son who knows and has experienced our pain. He is asking us to join with him in his passion for fallen mankind. He knows what we feel even greater than we do. He has experienced the fullness of our loss. He, too, was deeply wounded and felt every tear that our wounds produced.

When we resort to looking for the goodness and comfort of God, our pain will bring on new dimensions. What was made to be evil, God makes good. When the waters of evil rise to their peak, not only is God good, but he is also extraordinarily better. He will take the evil surrounding death and bring much good out of it. Love overcomes death! Incredibly, I find myself saying:

Oh, God, I love you! I love you for bringing me to this place. Am I crazy? Somehow the closeness I now feel with you, God, is an intimacy I have longed for my entire life. It is, indeed, horrible to be here; yet, so very wonderful. Mornings with you are so fantastic, that I long to be in your presence every day.

Somehow, I know that you have allowed me to enter into a deep and personal place of pain and sorrow. Because I have lost a child, I have gained a new closeness to you. You have asked me to join you in your suffering. You experienced the death of your Son. You willingly let him die for the sins of man, my sins. In his death, you experienced all the pain and horror that we are facing in the death of our child. Your pain became the greatest moment of history. God gave us his Son. It was the moment of humanity's redemption. In your great love, you willingly sacrificed your Son.

Right now, I have much I would like to talk about with Marcie, mostly, about her new life, its splendor and majesty. When I lie in bed, I often ponder what is to come. I continue to search my heart and listen in the silence. I continue to believe in the goodness of God and how this intimate journey with pain guided me into his presence. My pain was not a physical pain but a spiritual cancer that longed for healing. It drew me to God's goodness, his kindness, his strength, and his love; a deep and incredible love I had never experienced before.

God Knows and Shares the Depth of My Suffering

During the visits of the great mass of people who came to the funeral home, one person said something that I should have known from all my experience in ministry. I had spent 30 years sharing this with others, but the time had come for me to know and understand this truth in a richer and more intimate way.

When I entered into this great sorrow, like many others who have had this experience, I didn't want someone giving me pat answers to try to alleviate my pain. Those who don't know the depth of this pain often make comments such as, "God loves you" or the clichés, "Everything will work together for good," "God had this all planned," and others. Those in deep pain feel a sense of revulsion when we hear these naive statements. More helpful would be truths about our compassionate and caring Father. I remember every person who came to the funeral. When I think of specific individuals, I usually recall the short time we had together and our brief conversations. Of all those interactions, however, I can't remember who shared this remarkable comment. I think that person may have been there just to tell me this insight and may not have been closely tied to Marcie.

The person simply said, "God knows what you feel." I probably thought, *Well, of course, he knows what I feel. He is, after all, the God of the universe who is omniscient.* But the person went on to say, "God, too, had a child die, so he knows what losing a child feels like."

That statement touched me at that time but not nearly as much as it would when I began to read about others' similar experiences. Describing the deepest insights into the depths of God's compassion for parents who lose a child, I was especially touched by an excerpt from Nicholas Wolterstorff's *Lament for a Son*[xi]. Nicholas had lost a son in a tragic accident.

> *How is faith to endure, O God, when you allow all this scraping and tearing on us? You have allowed rivers of blood to flow, mountains of suffering to pile up, sobs to become humanity's song: all without lifting your finger that we could see. You have allowed bonds of love beyond numbers to be painfully snapped. If you have not abandoned us, explain yourself. We strain to hear. But instead of*

hearing an answer we catch sight of God himself scraped and torn. Through our tears we see the tears of God. God is not the God of the sufferers, but the God who suffers. The pain and fallenness of humanity have entered into his heart. Through the prism of my tears I have seen a suffering God. His sorrow is his splendor. To redeem our brokenness and lovelessness, the God who suffers with us, did not strike some mighty blow of power, but sent his beloved son to suffer like us, through his suffering to redeem us from suffering and evil.

For the first time, I experienced God coming close and entering into my own suffering. He was no longer distant, a God of the past. He was present and was there to redeem me from my suffering because he knew and shared the depths of my sorrow.

Death is Our Enemy

Where, O death, is your sting? (1 Corinthians 15:55)

Some might say that God took Marcie. Not for one minute do I believe that. I think that gives the wrong picture of God. The reality is that death is our enemy, and death is God's enemy. In the book, *Denial of Death,*[xii] Ernest Becker explores the reality of death.

> *The fear of death is indeed, a universal in the human condition.*
>
> *Fear of death is universally present. Children become aware of it; it is terrifying and somehow locks in deep in our unconscious, but it continues to remain present to all thoughts. It is a mainspring of human activity—all of our activity is largely to avoid the fatality of death. It haunts the human animal like nothing else.* (from pp. 14-16)

Christ conquered death on the Cross! The Scriptures give us great comfort to not fear death and to be people filled with hope.

> *Since the children have flesh and blood, he too shared in their humanity so that by his death he might break the power of him who holds the power of death—that is, the devil— and free those who all their lives were held in slavery by their fear of death* (Hebrew. 2:14–15).
>
> *Yea, though I walk through the valley of the shadow of death, I will fear no evil* (Psalm. 23:4, KJV).
>
> *Death has been swallowed up in victory. Where, O death, is your victory? Where, O death, is your sting?* (1 Corinthians. 15:54b–55)

When American philosopher Dallas Willard, known for his Christian spiritual formation writings, was dying, he expressed full confidence in the Scriptures. His last words about his life and death were, *"Thank You"* (*Preparing for Death*, 254). We no longer have to fear death and can have the same assurance. We can be filled with gratitude in both death and life. So, with this confidence, I have learned to say "thank you" for both in my life.

Lessons from Our Dog, Laker

After 25 years of not wanting a dog, my son, Robert, finally convinced me that we should get one. The dog we chose, Laker, was a yellow Labrador Retriever, just like a dog you might see pictured on a calendar. Laker was adorable, like most puppies, but this one yellow, fluffy ball of energy grabbed my heart. Laker became a big part of our family's life and everyone that knew him—little children, adults and even strangers—loved him.

We started taking Laker to dog obedience classes. While Robert and I were attending our nephew's football game, we received a desperate call from Jeanne having to do with Laker. As our precious little puppy was going into class, a pit bull broke loose from his leash and attacked him. Jeanne, already at the end of her rope, found this to be way too much for her. When I returned home, I was furious. For the first time since Marcie's death, I exploded with anger. All of my frustration from the past year was exposed. Little Laker had cuts and scrapes all over him and was showing signs of the pain you might see in an emotionally abused dog.

The pain that Laker experienced that night traumatized him, and the effects lingered. Afterwards, when an angry dog would confront him, and we weren't quick enough to intervene, Laker would lie down defenseless and let the dog have its way with him. Just yesterday, nearly two years after his encounter with the pit bull, an angry dog attacked him. Laker just laid down and wouldn't fight back. We had to pick him up and put him in our truck. Laker would experience this kind of fear, even if a dog might not be aggressive. He was perfectly content to be with us and to be safe, rather than outside running around. Laker is a dog that loves life and is so happy when he can play with another dog. Yet the deep pain inflicted by the pit bull repeatedly caused him to pull back and to receive far less than life had to offer a healthy dog.

Many of us act similarly as a result of the scars we have received in life. We have loved living life to its fullest; but when hurt, we have gone and hid in safe places. As a result, we end up settling for far less than what life has to offer.

For many, the hurt and pain accompany death may result in a similar withdrawal from life. This is especially true with the death of a child. When you love a child unconditionally, with all your heart, and your child dies, the pain is so great that you become quite afraid to ever love again.

I think this is also true about many of life's greatest struggles. We want so much to be successful, and we try very hard. If high a mountain causes us to detour or lose our way, we get frustrated and depressed and may simply quit. The failure and resultant pain take away all of our motivation to try again.

I didn't know how to help Laker overcome his deep fear. I wanted so much for him to live fully and freely without it. I had no way to give him what he needed to heal. Perhaps, he just needed more love and acceptance from us.

For myself, I have found that unconditional love and forgiveness from the God of the universe frees me from any pain that might cause me to pull back from life. His unconditional love and forgiveness nurture and heal me as he allows me to fail, even when I pull back in fear. He gives me strength to be truthful about my failures and to get up and try again, no matter how often I fail or disappoint him or myself. God's love is always a love that grants second, third, and countless other chances. He so much desires for me to experience all the joy that life has to offer.

I remember these words that Jesus said, "I have come that they may have life and have it to the full" (John. 10:10b).

Our First Anniversary Without Marcie

When the fire is hottest, stand still

We are very close to the first anniversary of Marcie's death. The forces of evil, death, and destruction surround us. I started a new journal in the beginning of September, and my entry on the first page was written with much hope.

> *I am entering into a new pilgrimage. I don't know where it is heading, or how much it will be different, but I am feeling and hoping that a new day would come; a day that would free us from the assaults of the past months.*

The day that came was anything but a "new day." September became filled with deep trouble. Today, begins with me sitting on the porch at 5:45 in the morning. Still dark, the sun is beginning to rise. The trees are in bloom, yet I still have a full view of the moon, the sky, and one star, the star that I saw the night of Marcie's death.

I have just read John 1:1–4: "In the beginning was the Word, and the Word was with God, and the Word was God. . . . Through him all things were made . . . . In him was life, and that life was the light of all mankind. The light shines in the darkness, and the darkness has not overcome it."

Having an awareness of the immensity of the universe, the moon seems small, even though I know it is colossal. As I look at the moon and stars, I am reminded of the vastness of the universe. And I think, in the beginning, *GOD!!! WOW!* To see God as the Creator and Sustainer of this vast universe is to see how great and mighty God truly is.

Seeing the lushness of the vegetation flourishing from the considerable rain we had this past year, I feel assured of how blessed I am in this life and certain that the God of the beginning somehow loves and favors me. I am not bragging or boasting about his love for me, but I'm sharing it to let others know that he loves and favors all of us.

In *Traveling Mercies,* Anne Lamott describes the time she took her son to swim with seals. Anne much desired for her son to see the seals, but he was unable to swim far enough to get next to them. Anne cried out to God, for Christ's sake, do something. Miraculously, dolphins began to jump in every direction around the boat. As this happened, she recalls a fundamental religious principle: *God isn't there to take away our pain or suffering but to fill it with his Presence.*[xiii]

Faith believes that the worst thing that can happen is, always, the next to the last thing. So, don't tell others of your success or blessings; instead, tell them that God is faithful, strong, and loving. Our travail and sorrow have a purpose. A personal, loving God, who controls everything, makes sure of this.

Just moments ago, what I saw before me had been lit by only the light of my small feeble candle. Now, the sun has risen, and the light around me is radiant. In the upcoming days, I will need all this light and its energy to stand against the darkness that intends to surround me. September 2003 will become a month of many troubles.

My newest journey becomes a passage full of problems. September becomes a month of personal difficulties. Each day, I awake to yet another piece of bad news. It keeps coming. Blood is being spilled all around me. The sharks of evil smell it and are coming for the kill. This depth of trouble has left me without a clue as to all that is happening. I need help, and I need it badly.

First on the list, I receive word that a good friend of mine has been afflicted with a phobia, which so incapacitates him that he can't leave the area around his house. I hurt to hear that he is in such a desperate situation. At the same time, one of our staff members is diagnosed with severe, high blood pressure. His medical condition is very serious. And, sadly, one of our donors has just lost $600,000 in assets.

Then, Jeanne's paycheck was short by $2,000. This came at the worst time, as our cash was depleted from paying for school tuitions and books. We are, now, without enough funds to pay September's bills. Youth for Christ's finances are also depleted. Soon, we will have no cash left to afford the payroll. We have just received word that my niece, who has cancer, is beginning to fail. Reports of Hurricane Isabel, now category 5, loom in the distance. Striking at a lower level, but causing just enough damage, I have a severe ear infection again. Relentlessly, the anniversary of Marcie's death brings memories that cause deep sorrow and mourning. I am crushed by all the pain, yet life requires me to soldier on every day.

Reflectively, I start writing about the loneliness that I feel in my pain. I mourn because I feel that I am so alone on this journey. No one, really, wants to walk where I, now, have to. Sure, I have lots of friends who are great companions, but none whom I feel that can handle this level of despair. I am a lonely dancer, singing my song, walking my walk, dancing my dance, touching and inspiring. But when it all shakes down, I walk off the stage of life to go somewhere else, a place all alone, to suffer by myself. Last night, I was close to having a panic attack caused by the heat and sleep deprivation. I had nowhere to go to escape the sensation of claustrophobia caused by my sadness.

And the onslaught continues: Robert quits his job; a staff member's father is diagnosed with cancer; a very good friend's daughter is diagnosed with HIV. Overall, 22 significantly distressing events occurred in the month of September, none more significant, than the death of my niece. These events feel like carpet bombs we deploy to ravage Iraq and Afghanistan. Bombs are falling, falling everywhere; death and destruction abound. The onslaught comes from every direction, with no escape.

On Sunday, when I returned from church, I had an urgent message to call my sister. She told me that my niece, Lisa, had taken a turn for the worst and had just a few days to live. We immediately rushed to Winchester, Virginia to be with Lisa and her family. Seeing my niece on her death bed and watching her family and friends come to say their last goodbyes was deeply painful. She was unconscious, seemingly unaware of all that was going on around her. Yet when we prayed, for a moment, she seemed to acknowledge the words of the prayer she heard. The anniversary of Marcie's death was just a few days away. Could it be possible that Lisa would die on the same day that Marcie did?

Before long, I needed to leave Winchester and travel to Denver to be a part of an important conference for Youth for Christ executives from across the country. I wasn't sure if I should go, but I felt I needed to be a part of the event. The airport experience further increased my frustration. I had hoped to leave at 8:00 a.m., EST, and be in Denver by 11:00 a.m. to meet up with my good friend Darrell Scott, whose daughter had been killed in the Columbine School shootings. Over the past year, we had become good friends and brothers in the sorrow of the death of our daughters. Unfortunately, after a horrible experience with a delayed plane, causing my flight to arrive in Denver at 11:00 pm., I didn't make it to the hotel until the next day. After 19 hours of travel frustration, I never made it to see Darrell.

All in all, I enjoyed being with my many YFC friends. Unfortunately, the meeting itself was not as favorable as I expected because we learned that YFC/USA was in deep trouble. I left without much hope for its future nationally. But that was the least of my problems, for then I received word that Lisa had died—just one day before the anniversary of Marcie's death. So, I had to return to the pain of facing another funeral and also deliver the eulogy, while dealing with the deep sorrow I felt associated with the first anniversary of Marcie's death.

I realized that I needed to talk with someone who could make sense of the pain that was assaulting me. What we had been experiencing had to be the deepest of spiritual struggles. This was not a casual convergence of bad events but had to be a severe purposeful attack!

A few months after Marcie died, a lawyer who had heard of her death called me and told me he wanted to get together to talk. He had also known the pain of losing a child and could empathize with us. He shared two very strategic things with me that day. First, he reacquainted me with the book of Job. Second, he gave me a book to read by Walt Henrichsen, an author whose writings helped form a foundation for my 30-year ministry to students. Walt had walked deeply with God and had been a student of his Word for many years. His book, *Thoughts from the Diary of a Desperate Man: A Daily Devotional*, is about his child who had died. I read it, over and over, and it ministered deeply to my soul.

According to God's sovereign plan, Walt was going to be in town in a few weeks. I called my lawyer friend and asked if he could arrange for me to meet with Walt. It proved to be a very significant time that I will never forget.

When I told Walt everything that had happened over the past year, and, especially, over the past month, he quietly listened. He didn't seem overly concerned about the implausible events. After I finished, I asked him what he thought.

Walt very cautiously formed his response, letting me know, repeatedly, that he wasn't sure why God puts some people through amazing pain. He floored me by, next, saying what he suspected was happening: "I think you are in this situation, because God trusts you." What?! I was astonished, honored, and amazed. How could this be? God trusts me?!

Then I asked Walt what he would do if he were in my situation. With much confidence, he clearly stated, *"You don't have to do anything; just hold on!"*

For several days, these insights continually would come to my mind: banish anxiety and worry; cease striving and know that I am God, the loving, kind, and omnipotent God!

> *God is our refuge and strength,*
> *an ever-present help in trouble,*
> *Therefore, we will not fear, though the earth give way*
> *and the mountains fall into the heart of the sea,*
> *though its waters roar and foam,*
> *and the mountains quake with their surging* (Psalm 46:1–3).
>
> *The Lord Almighty is with us;*
> *the God of Jacob is our fortress* (Psalm 46:7–8).

God is a silent God. He is silent because he does not need to speak. He does not need us to come to the rescue. He reigns, and he reigns in power. He sends his love and faithfulness. He confidently, quietly, and powerfully rules the universe. He does not need to act. His sheer presence is action. God doesn't require heroic actions on our part, just our willingness to trust him, to believe in his goodness, to accept his omnipotent love, and, in faith, to wait for his deliverance. The longer we can hold out, the bigger the victory!

When the fire in your life is the hottest, stand still!

Marcie's Appearance to Those Dying

I read the book, *Final Gifts: Understanding the Special Awareness, Needs and Communications of the Dying,* written by two women who had been hospice nurses for 15 years. Maggie Callanan and Patricia Kelley share many stories of what happens when people ar4 about to die. Those near death often have very close people in their past appear to them. A very thin veil stands between heaven and earth. Often, relatives and friends will become present and be seen, at times, called out by name.[xiv]

Marcie often would comfort those in pain. And we told several stories about Marcie appearing to some of our close friends and relatives.

One encounter was with our close friend, George Bernier, who was under hospice care. He told his wife that Marcie had appeared to him and told him not to fear. Shortly after hearing George's story, we heard that when Jeanne's uncle lay dying, and was not fully conscious, yet he reached out his hands and called out to Marcie.

Another confirmation of Marcie's presence came from my friend, Donna Martin. Her mother, Marge, was only hours away from death, so Jeanne decided to drive to Donna's mom's home in Rehoboth Beach, Delaware. Jeanne had an overwhelming feeling that Marge didn't have much time left and that she needed to be there to help and support the family. Marge had been in and out of consciousness all day and struggling with moments of panic and fear. She didn't seem aware of what was happening, and not being able to comfort her was sheer torture. That evening when Jeanne arrived, Marge very consciously looked at her bedroom door and said with a giant smile, *"Marcie, what are you doing here?"* She spoke those words with a childlike enthusiasm, as though seeing someone who had been away a long time.

The biggest mystery is that Marge had never met Marcie, but she embraced her presence as if she had just seen her long-lost friend. Winnie, Donna's sister, looked at both Jeanne and Donna and said, *"Who is Marcie?"* With tears and awe in their eyes, they explained that Marcie was Jeanne's daughter who had passed away. They were all so comforted at the thought that Marge had seen something beautiful, something beyond understanding; but whatever she saw, they could sense that she felt a great sense of peace. They saw it in her face, as the deep lines of anguish seemed to melt away.

No one knew what Marge and Marcie shared in that exact moment; but what was exchanged was beautiful. It reminded us that between the veil of life and death, God sends those who love us, and those who will comfort us, in our extreme times of fear and sadness.

One very special time I recall a great sense of Marcie's presence came at one of our YFC student conferences. I became close friends with Darrell Scott. Darrell's daughter, Rachel, was one of the students who had been killed at Columbine High School. You might remember that she was asked by one of the shooters, who had been her friend, just before being shot, if she still believed in Jesus. Rachel answered, *"You know I do."* Darrell came up to us after he had spoken at the conference. He told us, he had felt a great sense that Marcie and Rachel were present, and that they were very proud of what we were doing. I, too, felt that same amazing presence.

You might be skeptical about this, but that is okay. Yet I must say that somehow beyond our reasoning, the dead can be very present. If you open yourself up to this notion you, will find in your mourning that they have been present to you also. I don't know how this can happen, but it does.

Getting Personal

Being with someone during his or her last days of life on earth is a very holy time. God is very present, and those who have experienced this found it to be an important time spiritually. It is a time to not fear death but to be alert to what God is doing. If we open our eyes of our heart, we will be amazed.

During this time, we can see God in ways that we could only experience in the presence of death. After years of experiencing people dying, hospice nurses tell us to believe that, regardless of the dying person's physical state, what he or she is experiencing is very real. Drugs do not create this experience. Instead, it's a supernatural encounter as they pass on to the next world.

This is what Dallas Willard said on his deathbed. In his book that he wrote as he was dying, he told his co-author Gary Black that it was like he was seeing a hallway between earth and heaven with amazingly marvelous people in the hallway.[xv]

Grant's father's experience with a "little man" is an amazing story. And it is a great example of what can occur when people are dying. Everyone's experience is different. When we are with people who are dying, we are in a very holy moment, maybe the most holy moment we will ever encounter in our lives.

The Thin Veil
by Grant Grasmick

He was one of a kind—unique in many ways and a product of growing up during The Great Depression. My father was a self-made man who dropped out of school at the age of twelve to serve newspapers and provide for his family. When his father died of a sudden heart attack, it was left to my dad to fill his shoes, despite the fact, that he was the youngest of four siblings. But he had no choice. Upon returning from the funeral home, they found a placard attached to the front door of the house that read, "Eviction Notice." How much worse could things be for a young boy? You've just lost your father, an eviction notice is plastered over your front door, and you realize that your childhood is over. School is essentially finished for you at eighth grade, and you have to put food on the table for your family. Talk about coming of age!

Growing up, my father worked at numerous blue-collar jobs to make ends meet. He had a brief stint in the military, became a professional baseball player, and bought a business—from two elderly men he worked for—that he re-created in his own fashion. He came to know many politicians, businessmen, and celebrities but never forgot his roots. He was just as comfortable with the local stevedores working along the Baltimore waterfront as he was visiting The White House. In short, you would have to say they broke the mold with my father. And, although I am his only offspring, many young kids looked up to Dad as their second father. He coached dozens of boys through the years, from Little League baseball all the way up to college and offered summertime jobs to many more. He was always trying to instill a strong work ethic and competitive nature, which he felt would serve them well throughout life. And it did.

This is the briefest of histories for a man who lived until his early nineties. But it hopefully gives a bit of context to the flip side of his life in those final days. As you may gather, the "Depression Mentality" never really left my father. Regardless of how successful he became, I think he still felt somewhat insecure about the whole thing, understandably so, given his childhood experience. And that's what makes his "end of life" experience even more remarkable.

Dad was at work with me one day when he simply could not get out of his chair. No one knew what was wrong. But a battery of tests determined that he had pancreatic cancer. He was asymptomatic and totally without pain, which made things even more perplexing. But the test results did not lie, and the reality was, that he was in grave health. When we inquired of the doctors about his long-term prognosis, they felt he probably had a couple of months to live. This was not easy to accept, as it seemed he had a history of beating the odds. He had survived everything from open heart surgeries to carotid artery surgery, to prostate cancer surgery, and more. He was tough as nails. Yet, there we were, staring the Grim Reaper in the face.

What makes my father's death unusual to me? After all, according to the *United Nations World Population Prospects* report, approximately 7,452 people die every day in the United States. In other words, a person dies in the U.S. approximately every twelve seconds. So, death, in and of itself, is nothing out of the ordinary. But to me, his last couple of days were both distinctive and profound. Not every day do we hear someone talk about "the little man," but I will tell you exactly what I witnessed in that regard.

As things were winding down, my custom was to leave the office each day, and head to the hospital to visit him for a couple of hours or so. One day, in his "depression mentality" state, my father told me he thought he could still get out of the hospital, one more time, and make the family a bit more money. To this, I responded, "Time out." I told him that he was quite literally at "the finish line," and unless I had a fatal car accident on the way home, his race was going to be completed very soon, well before mine. In fact, I said to him, "You are at the finish line, and you are not leaving this hospital." I also told him that I appreciated everything that he had done for our family, but that the money, the business, and all those considerations meant absolutely nothing at this time. I asked, "Has it occurred to you, that in a very short period of time, you will be standing before your Creator?" He was silent, with no retort. I left him with that question to ponder for the evening and made my way home. This is where things got very interesting.

The following day, I went to the hospital after work, and he asked me to sit at the foot of his bed. He had something to tell me. We were on the third floor of Johns Hopkins Hospital, and he wanted to tell me what had happened after I had gone home on the previous evening. He said to me, "Last night, a little man came through that window. And he took me to the most beautiful place I have ever been in my life, beauty beyond description. The people I encountered were so loving. I have never seen anything quite like it."

I was dumbfounded and really had to ask myself if he had been hallucinating. But he was absolutely without pain and was not taking opioids. He was lucid. I pressed on and wanted to know if he was awake or asleep when the "little man" appeared. He wasn't quite sure. He only knew that the person was real and that he (the little man) had been taken away to a place beyond this world. He said that everything was absolutely fine and that my father had nothing to worry about. This came from a man who worried frequently. My father didn't quite know what to make of it. Neither did I, but he asked me for my take on the situation.

I told him, in no uncertain terms that I, absolutely, knew where he would be going when he died. He was going to heaven. I made this pronouncement because I had specifically asked him prior to his open-heart surgery, over thirty years ago, if he wanted to accept Jesus Christ as his Lord and Savior, and he did. So, I told him, unequivocally, that he was going to heaven, not because of anything he had done but because of what Jesus had done for him on the Cross. His sins were now forgiven, and his eternal destiny was assured. I believe, I left the hospital room more impacted that evening, than he had been as a result of my question the previous night. It was incredible.

The next day, I came back to the hospital and, again, was asked to sit down at the foot of the bed. My father rolled his eyes at me and simply nodded his head. And I asked, "What?" He nodded once more, so I asked, "The little man? Did he return?" Apparently, he had for the second straight night. Again, my father asked what I thought. And I told him, I believed he had witnessed a precursor to heaven. In essence, "the thin veil" had been drawn back, giving him a vision of where he was going. I told him that I couldn't say for certain if it was a vision or a dream, but one thing I knew was that he was not hallucinating because he was not taking medications. Within a week, he was gone— not, two months, as the doctors had predicted; it went much quicker. We had an amazing send-off for him, as the funeral service was really one of celebration. But that wasn't quite the end of the story.

Within a week or two after the funeral, I randomly opened my Bible and began reading Job 33. I am not sure why, but, apparently, I needed to read this chapter for a very specific reason. God had something in store for me, as the following words leapt off the page.

"But I tell you, in this you are not right, for God is greater than any mortal.

Why do you complain to him that he responds to no one's words?

For God does speak—now one way, now another—though no one perceives it.

In a dream, in a vision of the night when deep sleep falls on people as they slumber in their beds, he may speak in their ears and terrify them with warnings, to turn them from wrongdoing and keep them from pride, to preserve them from the pit, their lives from perishing by the sword.

"Or someone may be chastened on a bed of pain with constant distress in their bones, so that their body finds food repulsive, and their soul loathes the choicest meal.

Their flesh wastes away to nothing, and their bones, once hidden, now stick out.

They draw near to the pit, and their life to the messengers of death.

Yet, if there is an angel at their side, a messenger, one out of a thousand, sent to tell them how to be upright, and he is gracious to that person and says to God, 'Spare them from going down to the pit; I have found a ransom for them—let their flesh be renewed like a child's; let them be restored as in the days of their youth'—then that person can pray to God and find favor with him, they will see God's face and shout for joy; he will restore them to full well-being.

And they will go to others and say,

'I have sinned, I have perverted what is right, but I did not get what I deserved.

God has delivered me from going down to the pit, and I shall live to enjoy the light of life.'

"God does all these things to a person—twice, even three times—to turn them back from the pit, that the light of life may shine on them.

"Pay attention, Job, and listen to me; be silent, and I will speak.

If you have anything to say, answer me; speak up, for I want to vindicate you.

But if not, then listen to me; be silent, and I will teach you wisdom" (Job 33:12–33).

Call it "a dream" or a "vision in the night." Call him "a messenger," "an angel" or even "a little man." The point is that *God does speak*, and he specifically spoke to my father. He gave us all comfort, and he renewed our strength. He gave us hope and encouragement. The "thin veil" was indeed lifted, and because Jesus lives, we will live as well.

Again, Scripture says in 1 Corinthians. 15:21–22, "For since death came through a man, the resurrection of the dead comes also through a man. For as in Adam, all die, so in Christ all will be made alive." Thank you, Jesus!

How I know Grant

Grant and I have been friends for over 20 years. During that time, we have met on a regular basis and discussed many of life's triumphs and challenges. He has played a major role in helping Metro-Maryland Youth for Christ expand its ministry and has helped reach more and more of today's youth. His father was first involved in MMYFC starting in the 70s. Grant is one of the most committed men I have ever known and has a great compassion and commitment for expanding the work of God's Kingdom.

PART III
Letting Sorrow Become Your Friend

Introduction to Part III
Letting Sorrow Become Your Friend

In the story of the prodigal son, from the gospel of Luke, the climax comes when the prodigal son returns home. After receiving his inheritance, the son leaves and squanders his life. As the money runs out, and things turn for the worst, he finds himself feeding pigs and working as a servant. In that culture, this would have been the lowest of jobs, and he would have held no respect.

We would think that if he had thought about what his life should be like, he would have been motivated to return home. But he was afraid because he had wasted all he had received. His father's judgment would surely be too much to bear. When he, finally, runs out of options, he is forced to go home.

How would you expect the father to respond? We would expect him to scold and chastise the boy for the error of his ways. The greatest surprise of the story is that the father runs to greet his son upon his return and embraces him with no lectures or judgment. The father is overwhelmed with joy to, once again, see his wayward son. He quickly restores the son's place in the family by giving him a new robe, putting a ring on his finger, and adorning his feet with sandals. Instead of disgracing the prodigal, the father orders his servants to throw a big party to celebrate his son's return.

At first read this story, we may think the real change occurred when the son appeared to repent while feeding pigs. But the real transformation came when the son received his father's unconditional embrace and love. This is a great example of how sorrow can become our friend. When we try to stay away from the pain of sorrow, it continues to have power over us. When we draw near to it and embrace it, we find that sorrow does not desire to harm us but wants to transform us. The deep, warm presence of sorrow will liberate us from its grip (the fear of it).

Entering into Your Great Sadness

Sorrow is one of the key thoughts we must learn to take captive. As we become silent in our hearts and explore our sorrow, we become more aware of great moments and movements toward liberation and spiritual healing. Looking back on my life, I see a tapestry of death and sorrow. So much of it was a preparation for the great sadness that I would face in Marcie's death and its effect on our family.

One of the most powerful moments was when I heard author Joseph Bayly speak at a Youth for Christ Conference. Joe was a big man with a powerful presence of the Lord. His story about the death of his sons was something that I will never forget. It was the first time that I had encountered the concept of a "dark night of the soul."

Three of his seven children had died at young ages. Joe was intimately acquainted with the pain of death, and all too familiar with, what he once called, the enemy's "grim violence." But he was even more intimately acquainted with the One who conquered that enemy forever.

The View from a Hearse: A Christian View of Death (Also titled *The Last Thing We Talk About*)[xvi] is Bayly's simple and helpful meditation on death and grieving. He wrote it for those facing the death of a loved one, those still in the throes of grief, and those preparing to die. Joe knew that peace with death doesn't come from understanding everything that happens to us but in knowing the God who is in control of everything.

The presence of God in Joe's life was powerful, and his story is captivating. This remarkable presence was one that I recognized in many others who had experienced a deep encounter with suffering and death. The most transformational events that happen in our lives, occur when we invite God to walk with us through suffering.

As I listened to Joe, one of the lessons I learned was that sorrow can become our friend. When we are faced with the death of a loved one, we have two options: try to avoid and deny our suffering or draw close to it.

The problem with denying suffering is that it allows death to hold all the cards, and sorrow moves deeply into our soul.

Those who try to avoid facing the sorrow can take whatever life is left within them, often, then, living joyless lives.

The other option is to draw sorrow close and let sorrow become our friend. When I encountered my great sadness, I purposefully entered into my past experiences with Marcie through contemplation. In contemplation, I became fully aware of all the times we had spent together. As Joe had pointed out about mourning, we need to draw close to our sorrow by entering into, at least, three encounters dealing with the heart-rending event, in order to overcome, and be free from its effects. The first encounter involves experiencing deep pain. As we continue to move further into the event, our sorrow becomes less and less painful. Eventually, the pain will become our friend, and result in healing.

A healing experience for me was revisiting our vacations and the time we spent in Holden Beach, NC. For the past forty-two years, our family had taken vacations together. In the first few years after her death, we would go to the Myrtle Beach neighborhood where Marcie had lived and walk through her community. While quite painful, we also felt a sense of warmth. At the time, we were touching on something quite significant. It was as if Marcie's presence was with us. To be able to feel her warm presence was something very important in our healing.

Each morning, as I spent time in contemplative prayer, God would lead me to different events in Marcie's life and in mine. It was terribly painful every time. Yet I came to realize that it an important time that allowed me to move into deeper healing. I would walk through the many good times we had together, and my numerous times of failure experienced with Marcie. God's love and power was present in each and every encounter. Sorrow, eventually, became a great friend!

Sorrow Is a Prolonged Heartbeat

I'm living with constant sorrow. I have known sorrow all my recent days.

As we got into our van to go to the funeral, our children were playing a song by Brooks & Dunn that would pretty much sum up the days, weeks, months, and years ahead: "The Long Goodbye."[xvii] This surely would be a painful, long goodbye that would not end once the funeral and burial occurred. We would face many tough days ahead. Much sadness would follow us through all our days, more sadness than we could ever imagine at that moment. The shock of all that occurred has protected us from the full experience of losing Marcie. We could never have faced it all at once.

Whenever I think of Marcie, my heart fills with sadness. But even as this sadness fills my heart, I am committed to always remember her. If I must have sadness to think of Marcie, then I am willing to be sad. No parent would ever want to forget his or her child. So I must think of Marcie, and of the great moments we shared. I must let all the memories enter my heart, including the memories of sadness and grief.

I think of the days when we walked on the beach and our conversations began to feel like two adults sharing ideas. We began talking about life the way I like to talk about it, philosophizing about its meaning and dialoguing back and forth. Surely the days and times of the future would draw us deeper into our conversations. Marcie was always a deep-thinker, and she spent a lot of time talking to her friends about life. Those days ended; in their place, I know only loss.

When I think of our planned future visits with Marcie at Myrtle Beach, I am also left with sadness. Marcie so loved for us to be at her place, her town, showing us what her life had become and including us in her plans. The future visits were never to be, all doomed by the genetic condition known as qtc prolongation. More than a diagnosis, it had become a prolonged heartbeat that was the beginning of our long goodbye. It daily stirs the sense of loss and sadness in our hearts.

Let Death and Sorrow Become Your Friend

Perhaps all the dragon in our lives are Princesses who are only waiting to see us act, just once, with beauty and courage. Perhaps everything that frightens us is, in its deepest essence, something helpless that wants our love. " From *Letters to a Young Poet* by Ranier Maria Rilke.[xviii]

Most have an overwhelming sense that death is something to be feared and not to be discussed. We hope that if we avoid talking about death, it will go away. Unfortunately, the more we try to avoid that reality, the larger and more troublesome it becomes.

Growing up in a small town, we knew everyone that lived there. We knew when a stranger came to town. We would keep that person at a distance and feared their differences. But as we allowed the stranger to become our friend, we found that our differences could open a whole new world, a world that would make our lives more complete.

The key is to allow the sorrow of death to become our friend. If we begin to come close to it, it loses its dark power and it begins to become a healing force in our lives. Everything we fear can transforms us. James Hillman says, "It becomes convincingly clear that in order to become fully human beings, we have to claim the totality of our experience; we come to maturity by integrating not only the light, but also the dark side of our story into our selfhood" (Henri Nouwen, *Daily Meditation*, September 17).

Most people with whom I have discussed this express that they thought that being with someone who is dying would be dreadful. But they discovered that when they were with a dying loved one, they found that it to be one of the most powerful experiences of life. They entered into a holy place.

Recently I was with a wife and her children who were staying faithfully at the bedside of her husband as he approached his final hours. The children sang worship songs and shared with their father their thoughts of love and admiration for him. Then quietly as they sat at his bedside, his wife read aloud an Irish poem on death. The husband and father whose body was completely devastated and crippled by disease, sat up almost as if he were being lifted. He stared intently at something as if he had found great comfort and peace from his suffering—the peace that can only be found in God. At that very moment, the life left his body, and he died.

The family has expressed that being with him in these final moments is something they will never forget. It has become one of the most powerful spiritual experiences of their lives.

*When the perishable has been clothed with the imperishable, and the mortal with immortality, then the saying that is written will come true:
Death has been swallowed up in victory*
(1 Corinthians 15:54).

My Memories of Marcie

A helpful way of letting sorrow become our friend is by taking time to remember the experiences you had with your loved one. We should enter into these encounters by remembering the shared moments and experiences. This help release us from the fear of sorrow.

Here are some of my greatest memories of Marcie. As I was growing up, my favorite sport was basketball. It, also, became one of my family's favorite sports. Obviously, I wanted my children to play basketball too. When Marcie turned 6, we had her sign up to play. It turned out to be a disaster. As the kids were throwing the ball to each other, Marcie missed it, and it hit her in the face. She had enough, and she never, again, wanted to play.

A few years later, I was able to get her to try basketball again. She was interested because her friends were playing. She had great success and enjoyed it. When she was 12, I became her coach. When we played for the championship, I had Marcie guard the best player in the league. She played an amazing game, and we won!

Marcie was never one who was too intense with athletics. She made the soccer team at McDonogh High School and was one of the stars on the J.V. team. This gave her an opportunity to play for the Baltimore Soccer Club, one of the top club teams in the area. Although she enjoyed it, in her sophomore year she switched to playing volleyball for McDonogh. Because of her love of the game, Marcie's sisters, Julie and Vee, both played four years of volleyball, joining the year-round volleyball club teams as well.

Marcie was an amazing person all around! She was great at choosing unique and perfect presents. For my birthdays, I remember Marcie giving extravagantly. They were such perfect gifts, and often she couldn't afford them. When my first birthday after Marcie's death arrived, I felt the profound absence of the gift she was to us. Future holidays, birthdays, vacations, her visits home, and lunches together during those visit—all that was gone. And as each event occurs, sorrow and sadness fill the void.

Marcie also loved to draw. One of my most treasured drawings is her incredible self-portrait. I am still amazed at how she captured her own beauty.

She also loved listening to music. I remember sitting in our club basement together, when Marcie was in kindergarten, listening to Willie Nelson. Her favorite song was, "Mommas Don't Let Your Babies Grow Up to Be Cowboys." Her version was, *Mommas Don't Let Your Daughters Grow Up to Be Cowgirls*. We often laughed when she would sing loudly, changing the lyrics to suit her fancy.

Another fond memory took place on a remote island in the Bahamas. We were invited to do a retreat with students, and Marcie came with us. She quickly became the star of the retreat. She was the first one to make friends and know all the students by their names. She threw herself into the life of each student with an enthusiastic love. Her smile and friendliness were contagious.

When I was in college, I longed to live my life at the beach. At one point I was considering dropping out of school and going to Mexico. Living at the beach was never a dream that came true for me, but, interestingly, in Marcie's short life, she was able to live my dream. She vacationed in Aruba, Cancun, the Bahamas, St John's, and a number of the Caribbean Islands. After she finished college, she was living in Myrtle Beach, and she needed to get a job. Jeanne was scheduled to meet Marcie in Myrtle Beach the week after she died to help Marcie get a job with her company. After Marcie's death I remember seeing a picture of her on the beach. I was comforted to know that her next vacation was on the beaches in Heaven.

Oh, how we miss Marcie—in everything we do and everywhere we go. We will never forget how we were blessed by her presence and all the wonderful times we shared. We will cherish these moments forever. Going back and remembering the many time we had together, both good and bad, have been very beneficial in helping me deal with her loss.

A picture of Marcie and me during our family vacation in July 2002 at Holden Beach, NC. The beach is a place filled with many summer memories.

Marcie's Self-Portrait

McDonogh High School

This morning, I have an appointment with my ear doctor, whose office has relocated next to McDonogh School. As I drive on Greenspring Avenue, I am reminded of Marcie's school days. What a wonderful opportunity Marcie had as a student there.

McDonogh is situated on rolling hills in one of the more beautiful parts of Baltimore. It has great history, and its buildings declare it. Its academics are some of the finest. Besides attracting some of Baltimore's most prominent and wealthy families, it also attracts some of Baltimore's top students. Marcie had received a full, academic scholarship to attend. True to her nature, she was, ever and always, her own person. Marcie unconditionally loved her fellow students for who they were, not on the basis of their wealth or prominence. The students at McDonough mutually loved Marcie because they knew her to be a real, authentic person.

Jeanne often tells the story of the day Marcie visited the school as a prospective student. We, especially Marcie, really weren't aware of McDonogh's history or prestige. For our visit, Marcie was dressed in tattered jeans, converse sneakers, a T-shirt, and flannel shirt over top. She definitely wasn't concerned about being dressed to impress. That was part of Marcie's carefree attitude.

In the fall of her junior year, Marcie made a huge mistake, one that almost got her expelled from the school. It was devastating to our family that she might lose this incredible opportunity.

Marcie called us on a Friday to tell us what had happened. Apparently, she had a close friend who was having a difficult time coping with life. The friend was spending a lot of time drinking to avoid the pain she felt. Being the caring, young woman, she tended to be, Marcie was more than willing to help her friend deal with her life.

Unfortunately, Marcie's judgment was significantly impaired in her desire to help. She brought some wine to school for her friend to consume over the weekend. This friend, however, drank some during school and was caught in the act. Although her friend didn't expose who had supplied the wine, Marcie went forward and admitted her guilt.

Obviously, for what she had done, Marcie deserved to be expelled. We realized this and accepted it with considerable pain. In hope against hope, we prayed that somehow Marcie would be able to remain at McDonogh. Like all families faced with this kind of problem, we were in deep angst. Adding insult to injury, we were supposed to be a model Christian family that didn't have those kinds of issues. We would have to live with that stigma as well. But we hoped and prayed that Marcie could stay at McDonogh somehow. We decided to be open about this situation with our friends, and many were praying for us.

That Monday evening, we were meeting with the headmaster, preparing to face the consequences. We knew that we could not do or say much. We had to face the consequences and were expecting that Marcie would be expelled.

We were waiting to see the headmaster—the other girl's parents' meeting occurred first. When they came out, they gave us a look to expect the worst!

We went in and apologized for what had happened and did not give any excuses for Marcie's behavior nor try to convince the headmaster to give her another chance. We were sorry for what had occurred and apologized for Marcie not valuing the opportunity that McDonogh had given us. We listened as the headmaster and his assistant informed us of their position.

The headmaster was taken aback because he couldn't believe our attitude. He was accustomed to parents who defended their children and their rights, trying to manipulate the situation to their advantage. To our surprise, he commented that we were the kind of parents that he looked for to be a part of the McDonogh community. Furthermore, he told us that maybe something could be worked out for Marcie to stay—no promises, but he would see.

The next day, Marcie and I arrived at school to clear out her belongings. This would, probably be the last time she and I would be at McDonogh. Instead, it turned out to be one of the most unbelievable experiences I have ever had. It was the first time that tears of sorrow were turned into tears of unexpected joy, as Marcie was recognized for the person she truly was.

Something short of a quiet demonstration was underway on the McDonogh campus, involving Marcie's potential dismissal. One teacher shared about a cloud of darkness that seemed to hang over Marcie's English class. To the extent, he told us, of not being sure if one of his students would survive Marcie's dismissal.

When the students realized that Marcie was on campus, they began to approach her. They reassured her that they were willing to do anything to keep her there. As we were leaving, our car was mobbed with students who were all trying to assure Marcie of their support!

I sat next to Marcie in our little Nissan Sentra crying deep tears of joy. When she asked what was wrong, all I could say was, "Marcie, you are amazing. I can't believe it. This is incredible!" Marcie was a real person, and they knew she deeply cared about them. Those to whom she had been loyal, and had loved, were now rallying to her cause!

Within a few days, we heard from the normally stern headmaster that they were going to give Marcie a second chance. This grace was surely from the hand of God.

This predicament was a potential crisis that I will always remember. It gave me a picture of Marcie that I will continue to treasure. When I think about sitting in that car next to her, I can still feel the great love and loyalty she inspired in her fellow students. I often shed tears of joy for the great treasure that God gave us in Marcie. She was, forever, her own person. She loved people for who they were and never raised judgement. People felt this genuineness, and she was loved and respected for it.

An Emotional Challenge of a Lifetime

by Dr. Ian MacFawn

A year after the tragic death of his son in a Helicopter accident, Ian found a way to come to grips with his sorrow—by honoring his son and bringing closure to a tragic loss.

It has been a very difficult year, since my son Breandan's death on October 23, 2014. I see and feel how each person in our family has been strong through this tragedy, but it has taken its toll. We have been weakened and show our emotions more than ever before. We have been suspended over a very deep chasm by a bridge, a bridge of faith. Though now, we are emotionally helpless at times, the bridge holds and will support us. God is good.

I was on my way last year to a full Ironman Triathlon, the physical challenge of my lifetime, when Breandan's tragedy occurred. Instead of racing that day, I buried Breandan and began the emotional challenge of my lifetime. Breandan's last words to me offered an encouragement, in my quest last year, to accomplish that goal.

Tomorrow, I will try again to meet this physical challenge. Tomorrow, I will remember Breandan's encouragement to push me on; to help me get through the pain. I will try to finish with a smile and, I'm sure, a few tears.

God bless me and all of you. Thank you, for you.

How I know Ian

I first heard Ian's wife share her story about Breandan. When I saw later that Ian had posted this story on Facebook, I was so touched by this loving tribute to his son that I wanted it to be in my book. Cathy and Ian are dear friends of ours that live in Western Maryland.

A Note about Marcie
by Robert Arnold, Jr.

Death is defined as "the end of the life of a person or organism." The death of a loved one, or family member, is very stressful and can define someone's life. When you realize that you will never see or speak to this person again, it causes great pain. After the loss of my older sister, Marcie, I felt something I have never felt before—a feeling of helplessness, as if I could do nothing to change this situation.

Marcie had such a positive impact on my life; these feelings of despair did not last for long. I could not think of my sister in such a negative light. Marcie was such a positive, kind, and caring person. She was well liked by all her friends and family members. She was the type of person who would go out of her way to help someone who was feeling down or in need. I was fortunate to spend a lot of time with her during the last six years of her life. I cherish these years.

During the summer of 2002, I lived with Marcie in Myrtle Beach. Little did we know that would be her last summer with us. Marcie helped me find two jobs, let me borrow her car, took me out, introduced me to all of her friends, and allowed my friends to visit and stay at her apartment. She always checked in with me to make sure I was enjoying my summer vacation. Marcie and her friends would do anything for me if I asked.

When I think of all the memories and great times we had together, one always one always stands out. Marcie would tell me that she loved me and would insist that I tell her I loved her too. Marcie truly cared about me and the rest of her family and friends. You could always count on her for good advice or a helping hand. She taught me a lot about life and how to navigate through the tough times. I was truly blessed to have her as a sister and to spend that last summer together.

Always Never Here

by Douglas Mobray

You were born on a February day.
You were body gone on a September day.
I bore no witness to your birth;
I bore no witness to your death;
I bear witness to your life;
I bear witness to your everlasting life.

What physical proof I have
of our too-brief engagement
(remember when I asked you
to be engaged to be engaged to me?)
is stored in a box I keep with me
through all my moves,
through all my versions of me.
A handful of pictures,
a palmful of letters,
a small bounty of holiday greeting cards—
your words, constant constellations.
And a 7-second recording of your voice
on my answering machine one October day,
wishing me *happy birthday*,
offering me love and hope.

I still believe your love saved my life.
It is the only solid belief
I have ever held.
I have faith in the life
I now continue to live
is one of your countless gifts.

I cannot call you on the phone,
like I did for many years,
annoying you with my adamancy.
I cannot tell you how much
you mean to me

still mean to me,
in those same simple ways—
your address is eternity;
your place is within me.

I am talking to myself now;
but it is your voice I hear
when I am in need of comfort.

There is also comfort
in having no doubt
I was able to say
everything I needed to say,
for you to hear from my heart
the overflow of love I felt
when you were beside me,
before you were in the never not here.

I cannot remind you
of my gratitude the same way
someone tells another person
anything at all when both
are still in body motion.

I can only make this offering
and hope that some sliver
of this simple act
finds its way

and finds any piece of you
still vibrating in the universe
(even if and especially if
that place is within me).

The Pain Grows—I Must Never Forget Her

My heart is in anguish within me; the terrors of death have fallen on me.
Fear and trembling have beset me; horror has overwhelmed me.
I said, "Oh, that I had the wings of a dove! I would fly away and be at
rest.
I would flee far away and stay in the desert;
I would hurry to my place of shelter, far from the tempest and storm
(Psalm. 55:4–6).

The pain is especially deep this morning. Only a few months have passed since I experienced the trauma of the funeral. The intensity of the pain has grown so great that don't think I can live with it much longer. I must have some lessening of this anguish. Instead, each passing day, I come uncomfortably closer to the trauma of the death of my child. I feel the pain in greater ways. Oh, how I wish I could run and hide. But where can I go and not be followed by the pain?

Christmas is getting close, and we're expecting dreadful days ahead. How will we share this first Christmas without Marcie's presence? At this moment, every event since her death causes pain and a dark and heavy cloud of mourning.

Each year for the past 27 years, between Christmas and New Year's Eve, we have taken a group of students on a ski trip called, the *Living End*. Every time, it has been one of the most exciting, most anticipated youth ministry events. We had between 200 and 500 students attend annually. Many of the students were non-Christians who had never entered the door of a church. During this time, many students sought out Christianity and found hope in God's love. For a number of years, many of the students who attended were friends that Marcie had invited to our Campus Life youth group meetings. While there, she saw many of these same friends become Christians.

We had fun memories of Marcie learning to ski at these events. Once, when I was teaching her to ski, she suddenly slipped and lost control, nearly falling off the slope into some trees. She laid there helpless with her skis tangled and her poles askew. She looked up at me with those big brown eyes. She didn't complain, but I knew she wasn't very happy with me.

A deep sadness always seems to loom around the memories of the *Living End* event. A year ago, Marcie attended this with me. I remember us going to the movies, having dinner, and just hanging out. I loved having the adult Marcie with us.

This time, as I walk through the halls of the hotel, memories of Marcie surround me. I am closer and closer to the pain. Skiing, movies, and dinner—all these activities bring me nearer to my loss. It hurts so much and yet, mysteriously, something about the closeness of the pain feels comfortable and good. I must never forget Marcie!

I am reading *Holding on to Hope* by Nancy Guthrie.[xix] I am comforted by her words, "There are no easy answers. You must face grief head on, trudge through it, feel its full weight, and do your best to confront your feelings of loss and hopelessness with the truth of God's Word. You must come to the point of being truly human through your suffering and let that help you become more like Jesus" (p. 127). These words give me some hope because they help me understand the reality I am facing.

Last night, I woke up thinking: Will I remember Marcie in thirteen years? This question traumatized me. I do not know why 13 years is significant. But I cannot live with the thought that.

I could, or would, ever forget her. Will the passing of time lessen her importance to me? Today, every day since her funeral, the thought of who she was is so very precious. I want it always that way. No matter how bad the pain, this cherished closeness to Marcie must always remain.

I remember the day of the funeral, and how close I felt to eternity. At that time, I felt that only days, even hours, till, once again, we would see Marcie and rejoice. It was such a sweet and comforting thought. But as time has passed, it seems so far away. What especially hurts, is having to accept that many years may pass before we see her again—many days of grief, hurt, loss, and pain that we will have to pass through. So very many more days!

We had Marcie just long enough to never forget her. We had so many great times and deep conversations where we were just beginning to know her as an adult. *God, it hurts so much not to have her now. Help me, Lord, to release her to you. Teach me how to mourn properly. Somehow help me to remain healthy; to strike a balance between the joy of Marcie's life and the sorrow I am feeling from her death.*

I am reading just about everything I can read, especially by parents who have lost their children. They are great voices of comfort. When I read Gregory Floyd, *A Grief Unveiled*, his words became a great comfort to me as well. He helped me to understand some of the profound loss I feel with Marcie's death. I now realize the reasons I feel so strange is that part of my heart is not here anymore. I gave it to Marcie, and she took it with her. I can never again be totally whole, or at home, in this universe.

Also, I am reminded of the Apostle Paul's words: *Therefore we are always confident and know that as long as we are home in the body we are away from the Lord. For we live by faith, not by sight. We are confident, I say, and would prefer to be away from the body and at home with the Lord"* (2 Corinthians 5:6–8). Somehow, I must make it my goal to please him, whether I am at home in the body, or away from here and with him.

I know, now, that I will never live without this pain. To not have this pain is to not have Marcie in my heart. I choose the pain because I choose to always have Marcie as a part of my life. I could only avoid the pain by not thinking about her. I would never consider this. From now on, this pain will be a life companion. Somehow, I must come to know it as a friend. But for now, the thought of it being with me a lifetime is totally foreign. Never in all my existence would I think I would face this kind of pain that now overwhelms me. By some means, I know I must go face-to-face with it. In some way, I know that in its depth it will bring healing. I must not run from it. I must come to embrace it even though it will always hurt. Somehow, someday, I know that it will become a friend.

God's Ever-Present Help

I wait for the Lord, more than watchmen wait for the morning, . . .
[Bobby], put your hope in the LORD,
for with the LORD is unfailing love and with him is full redemption.
. . .

[Bobby], put your hope in the LORD, both now and forevermore
(Psalm 130:6–7; 131:3).

I stand shaken to the core of my existence by Marcie's death. Yet, in the midst of it I feel God standing with me, and I see his activity all around me. But I am like a wounded soldier, still reeling from the pain of the hurt but not yet seeing the healing. I am going to need considerable time to grieve and heal.

Several weeks after Marcie's death, I find myself crying from time to time. Yesterday morning, when Jeanne came downstairs and moved towards me, I cried uncontrollably. That Marcie is dead seems so unreal, yet each day the stark reality seems to grow closer. We have joined a unique club of people who have lost a child, a sibling, and a sister. Our whole family has been affected by this tragedy.

I have been looking, expectantly, for a supernatural daily visit with God. I anticipate him meeting our needs in a very present way. I hoped he would come rescue my family, and me, so that this great sorrow would disappear. Yet the grief continues to be prolonged. God is telling me something different. Instead, I am assured, that all I need to deal with in this crisis has been built into me over the past 40 years. God tells me, "You are capable, because I have made you capable." Fortresses are not built during times of trouble; they are built in times of peace.

Nonetheless, I see a great paradox within me. I find myself saying, *Oh, God, I love you for bringing me to this place that I longed for my whole life. It is a place of great intimacy with you. However, the way I got here is so horrible. Yet it is such a wonderful place to be. My only desire, now, is to be with you each morning.*

Four months have passed since Marcie's death. It seems like an eternity, for it has been filled to overflowing with intensity. Joy and sorrow are with us continually. It is a steady calling that God has invited us to enter.

The experience has been rich and very deep. Our lives have been broken by this death. It is a cut, a wound deep into our souls. We are on a journey that will bring healing and wholeness. The outcome is not clear at this time because it is a process, a road not traveled by us before and with no road maps. Our faithful companion, grace, provides only enough to face today. The past is gone, and the future is way too overwhelming to face. Only the present is possible.

We all will suffer. When we make the connection between Christ's suffering and ours, redemption will come. We worship a God who felt terror, abandonment, bewilderment, and loneliness and who was misunderstood, even by his friends. And he says to each of us, "Come to me, all you who are weary and burdened, and I will give you rest" (Matthew. 11:28).

The Presence of Two Bodies

Two bodies have taken over my life: the broken body of Christ on the Cross and the lifeless body of Marcie lying on the couch in Myrtle Beach. My life is wrought by these two broken bodies through suffering and healing. To remember this, I bought a large, beautiful gold cross while we were at the funeral home preparing for Marcie's funeral. That cross sits in the room where I daily read, pray, and meditate.

On the day of the funeral, Jeanne found, in our basement, an amazing photograph that taken by Marcie's high school boyfriend, Bo. What we saw in the photo was astonishing, yet another intimate message from God. The photograph was of Marcie lying on a couch sleeping. In the picture, we saw a glimpse of what we imagined Marcie's last moment was like; the moment she lay dying on her couch in Myrtle Beach. Her broken yet peaceful body was etched in our mind.

The grief from Marcie's death cuts deeply. It is always present and remains an open wound that will always be with me. Grief has caused me to taste deeply of death. In it, I have become aware that death is the ultimate reality, with the power to level anything we might hold of importance. This is especially true when one tastes the devastating death of a child.

Every morning, this sorrow has become the pathos that wholly influences my reading, thinking, and praying. It reminds me, that in my grief, Christ is present. His Father feels and knows my pain. His Presence reminds me that God is inviting me to unite with him in my suffering. It has created a union for me with him through the passion of Christ. It causes me to feel deep pain for the suffering of the world. My open wound helps me feel the pain of others. God is inviting me to connect my suffering with his suffering for the redemption of the world.

Jesus was led to the Cross. He embraced his Father's will to sacrifice his life for us. From his Father's hand, he received the Cross joyfully. God has given us his Son, the One who suffered for us. He is the one who experienced pain and understands ours.

Each morning as I pray and meditate, I feel the presence of both bodies: Christ's and Marcie's. I need the intimate presence of both. I must not run nor hide from either. The presence of both brings healing and strength. Two real life emotions accompany these bodies. Marcie's dead body brings great sorrow. The broken body of Christ brings great hope, so that one day our sorrow will turn into joy.

God whispers, through my reading, that only a heart that has been broken by love is able to love with his unfailing love. He is inviting us to join him in his passion for humankind. He is telling us that in our woundedness, we can become a healer for those around us. Only a heart that has been broken by love, can love with his love. Those who have been wounded are the great healers and lovers.

Good Friday at the Farm

As we approached the one-year anniversary of Marcie's death, we spent Good Friday at our farm in Western Maryland. This farm had been given to us as a gift after Marcie's death. I was there, making preparations for Holy Thursday and Good Friday. As a community, we would celebrate the Lord's Supper and enter into the passion and sorrow of Christ through a time of meditation.

To be here on this anniversary would be very fitting. Being in communion with the sorrow of Christ has led us to this day and to this farm. The death of my daughter, Marcie, had deepened our connection to the sorrow of Christ's death on the Cross. We believe that part of the reason God has led us to this farm was for it to become a place of quiet, a place to renew our souls, as well as a place where our sorrows will turn into joy. The farm has a tranquil and exquisite meadow that we named Marcie's Meadow It lays between the beautiful Potomac River and West Virginia mountains.

When someone loses a child, that mom or dad begins to understand the great pain that God experienced when he willingly offered his Son to die for the sins of the world. God felt every emotion that we live through. He experienced all the pain and humiliation that Christ suffered. He was present, in every sense, in Christ's suffering and death.

This became even more real for us when we saw Mel Gibson's great movie, *The Passion of the Christ*. For the first time, we were transported into the depths of the pain, emotion, and humiliation that Christ suffered on our behalf. We were overwhelmed by the experience. As I watched it, initially, I lost the nerve to look at the rest of the film, especially after the scene portraying the floggings and beatings of Christ.

When the movie came out, person, after person, came up to Jeanne to tell her that they saw her pain and suffering in the pain and suffering of Mary, the mother of Jesus. We were also transfixed by Mary and her suffering from an earthly standpoint. She was intimately present and also subjected to the horrific pain and suffering of her son. He was her flesh and blood and her first-born son. We share some of that same pain when we think of the death of our daughter. Yet we know

Mary's pain had surpassed ours, for she had also watched her son being humiliated.

Also fitting was that we would be here on this first anniversary with a very special community of friends. They had helped us through some very rough days. These friends had walked with us side-by-side and had shared our pain. Tonight, we would begin our meditation with a seder, thanking God for our liberation from suffering. We would share in communion, the broken body and blood of Christ. As hard as experiencing such sorrow has been, going through it with our friends mysteriously helped us to experience God's glory.

Woundedness

Marcie's death came suddenly. Death became a unique and painful friend. It would, from now on, accompany me for life. I have given death a new name and his name is *Woundedness*. I am not totally comfortable with this friend, and I am not sure I want him as a life companion. But, so far, he has proven to be a valuable friend for me. He is doing things with me and taking me places I would have never gone. Woundedness has taken me to a good and healthy place. Even though I still don't totally trust or understand it, I am beginning to feel comfortable with his presence and trust his direction.

Because of my woundedness, I feel as though I have new strength and power to help others. Wounded people have been given a particular gift, an added measure of compassion, greater insight into loss, and a special understanding that comes with experiencing woundedness, firsthand.

Wounded people, also, have a greater gift of healing and of brokenness restored because they have experienced both. Paraphrasing Paul in 2 Corinthians 1:4, "I have wounded you to help others." Jesus was wounded for our transgressions. He was bruised for our iniquities. No way can we gain a crown without a cross. The ultimate place of service is to focus on healing others. Through healing others, we are healed as well.

We desperately want to be healed and delivered from the power of woundedness, but it won't let go. In due course, woundedness will bring healing and deliverance but not through withdrawal. It will bring healing and deliverance only by staying in its painful presence. Real life involves death, and death involves the experience of suffering.

Woundedness is essential for us to appreciate grace. All suffering according to Teresa of Avila is, first, God's suffering. That is the ugly reality of my life right now. Theological clarity does little to touch our deep despair unless we take time to trust and understand the true meaning of our wounds. They can bring healing to, not only ourselves, but to others. If only we would realize that we are not alone in our suffering; we would recognize how God extended his grace to us in the midst of his own suffering. *There is no greater love.*

Tears are Good for the Soul

I have been crying for years, especially when I remember certain things about Marcie. I also cry at the slightest things, such as a sporting event when a team wins or when I see young people express great compassion for a young person with disabilities. I cry at marriages, and I cry about others' joys and sorrows. I cry about anything almost every day of my life. Crying has become a great expression of my emotions.

God promises to someday wipe away all our tears. Our suffering and sorrow are first God's suffering and sorrow. Jesus wept at the death of his friend Lazarus. He wept over the affliction of death and the suffering of his family. Jesus' tears gave us a glimpse of how the Father feels over our grief and suffering.

> *Weeping may stay for the night, but rejoicing comes in the morning* (Psalm 30:5b).

> And when that morning comes, *"He will wipe every tear from their eyes. There will be no more death" or mourning or crying or pain, for the old order of things has passed away"* (Revelation 21:4).

> *Those who sow with tears will reap with songs of joy* (Psalm 126:5

I believe tears have a continuing role in my healing. Of course, physically they help by releasing stress hormones, removing toxins, and lowering blood pressure. I also believe, however, that my tears are a direct release from much of my sadness. Tears help me release my grief, so I can live with an open heart. Weeping began in my heart and helped me share a great deal of my vulnerability. Crying give those of us who are suffering a space to unite in a common experience. Tears are a gift of grace from God. Saint Ignatius of Antioch appreciated tears as a spiritual consolation. He placed them among things, such as courage, strength, devotion, intense love, inspiration, peace, and quiet. My tears lead me into times of great faith, meaningful hope, and a deeper love for God.

Getting Personal

This is an amazing story about how, many years after the death of his son, Howard finally came to grips what he had denied for years and years. To see how Howard came to the place where he was able to accept his son's death is moving and encouraging. It was life changing for Howard.

Timing crucial in dealing with our deep sorrow. God is in no hurry, and we should not be either. Trying to heal quickly the deep wounds of loss can hinder our recovery. We must realize that God has our backs. So we should take all the time we need for us to accept our losses and move through our sorrows.

Stuck in Grief
by Howard Lucy

Our world was turned upside down on May 5, 1967, when David, our eleven-month-old boy, died after surgery to remove a cancerous tumor from his abdomen. I was not a follower of Christ at the time and, honestly, didn't know where to turn, or how to handle the death of our son. To put it mildly, I became extremely angry at God and completely turned my back on him. I questioned, why he would allow this.

So I did what I normally do—shut down and internalized it. Here are a few examples of how stuck I was. If my wife even mentioned David's name, I would get up and walk out of the room. If you asked me how many children we had, I would say two, Dianne and Beth, our two daughters. I couldn't acknowledge David.

This way of life continued for around twenty years. Even though I committed my life to Christ in March of 1980, I remained stuck and consumed in grief. But slowly, and lovingly, God worked on my heart. This began a series of small breakthroughs. I recognized that God loved David infinitely more than I ever could. Betty and I could begin to talk about David and his brief life. We talked about how God's hand had been upon us. I, now, could tell people we had three children and that our son, David, had passed away.

The first major breakthrough came in the mid-90s at a

Promise Keeper event. I saw a father come out of the crowd and run to the front near the stage to hug his son. I lost it and broke down sobbing. I heard a still small voice—I believe it was the Holy Spirit—say, "You miss him, don't you!" And for the first time in almost 30 years, I admitted that I missed my son.

God continued to bring an inner healing. I apologized to my wife and asked for her forgiveness for not being there for her as I should have been, so we could walk through the loss of David together. The final healing came as we were watching the movie, "The Shack." First, when Mac was looking through the waterfall and saw his daughter, I found myself leaning forward looking for David; and with tears running down my face, I knew that he was okay in the hands of our loving God. A second healing, I could identify with, was when Mac admitted that he had been stuck, consumed in his own grief.

Today, some fifty plus years later, we still miss David and don't understand why he had to die so young, but we rest in these three truths: God loves David, infinitely more than we ever could; he is safe in heaven with Christ; and because, by God's grace, we have put our trust in Christ and him alone, we will spend eternity with our son.

To God be the glory!

How I know Howard

Howard and I met in Youth for Christ many years ago. While working together, we have become close friends. He now spends half his time living in Florida and half in New York. I guess you could call Howard a snowbird. We stay in regular communication even though our lives have taken us to different locations. He shared this story with me when we were leading a retreat together at The Meadow. I knew, then, that his story needed to be a part of this book.

PART IV
Ways of The Heart - Paths to Peace and Freedom

Introduction to Part IV
Ways of the Heart—Paths to Peace and Freedom

Above all else, guard your heart; for everything you do flows from it
(Proverbs. 4:23).

Our sorrow, involving our loss, is centered in our hearts. Healing is focused in our hearts, also, as it struggles to understand. To know my heart, its ways and longings, has been the most beneficial resource for me in dealing with my pain.

I have spent many hours in the morning in silence, giving God the space to open my heart to his healing. Eventually, I became aware of how fear, shame, and anger function as the main weapons that evil uses to attack me. Understanding *the ways of the heart*, helped me to understand that sorrow can become my friend. This has helped me recognize that I must not be tempted to bear the *shame* that the past can bring. Also, knowing the ways of my heart has made me aware of the danger that the *fear* of the future poses to my spiritual health. My safe place is to be fully present in the present moment in the presence of the Holy Spirit.

Coming to know the power of the virtues of *faith, hope, and love* has given me the strength to fight for control of my heart. To understand their value may take some time, but believe me, they have tremendous power because they are constant reminders of how God is on our side and how he desires to bring a substantial psychological healing into our lives. *Countering each thought of fear, shame, and anger, with faith, hope and love, brings the richest spiritual blessings of truth, which overpowers despair.*

Getting Personal

Learning that his daughter had committed to suicide five years earlier was excruciating. But slowly, over many years, Tim came to grips with the difficulty and immensity of the journey, one that he would travel the rest of his life. It would take tremendous courage and resolve.

Tim has found a great source of comfort through ministering to Vietnam War veterans in his community. Serving others can help those who grieve deal with loss while, at the same time, assisting and comforting others. We know from Scripture that God comforts us in our trouble so we can comfort others in their troubles (2 Corinthians 1:4). We need to be careful, however, to not move quickly into the next stage by taking on a mission. We need time to heal before we are able to help others. Jumping in too soon may compound our pain. We should take time and ask God to lead us, in his timing, to where we can be most useful.

You Never Said Goodbye
By Tim Price

I love the Lord, for he heard my voice; he heard my cry for mercy.
Because he turned his ear to me, I will call on him as long as I live.
The cords of death entangled me, the anguish of the grave came over
me;
I was overcome by distress and sorrow.
Then I called on the name of the LORD: "LORD, save me!"
(Psalm 116:1–4)

Laura was my oldest daughter. From the day of her birth, she was a very sensitive person. As a baby, she was sensitive to sound, food, light, and touch. She loved touch, and many nights she would fall asleep on my chest; or later, she would fall asleep in the crib while I sat on the floor and held her hand. This sensitivity branched out to her being sensitive to the feelings of others. She gravitated to those who were lonely, isolated by peers, different looking, emotionally needy, and troubled.

At times, she was picked on and bullied along with them. She converted these experiences and interactions into poetry.

Laura loved Emily Dickenson. She grew in her Christian faith through her study of Scripture and in her relationships with other believers.

Laura questioned matters; it was how she learned. At times, as she grew older, our conversations sounded like arguments.\

She wrote letters and sent cards to all those she loved. In her teenage years, she suffered greatly. She was sexually abused by a church member. She hid this for about a year. Additionally, her pain was magnified by a lack of support from her church friends. Initially, this lack hurt her more than the abuse. But the abuse haunted her, isolated her, and filled her with fear and depression. A dark cloud hung over her. It never went away. I was patient. I prayed. I trusted God for her healing.

Distance. Our relationship suffered. Laura was in therapy for several years. She lived in fear, and the therapy seemed not to work. The therapist told me to be her father, not her therapist, and to refrain from encouraging her to speak about her fears and delusions.

Eventually, Laura was hospitalized. While there, she expressed anger at me for not protecting her. I apologized and asked forgiveness for my insensitivity, but we did not speak out of the presence of her therapist. There was still a distance. Then she decided she would take care of a social worker's cat while they went on vacation, after having said, "… I do not want to visit my parents, quite yet." Days later, I came home to a very short note, "Dad, I am messed up. When I get myself together, I will be back home." I held on to that note. Now, it has been 23 years. Those were her last words. I held on to the words, "I will be back." We waited. We prayed. We trusted God.

We sent presents on her birthday and at Christmas. We prayed for more than ten years that she would show up. We hired a private detective to find her and then would leave gifts at her door. When I left gifts for Laura, I would let her know that we would wait for her to call, write, anything, but would not violate her privacy. Weeks turned to months, months to years. We continued to leave presents at her husband's parents' home. We heard that she and her husband had moved to Charlotte. We found out that he worked there. We were told to stop leaving presents. We waited. We prayed. We trusted God.

Our hopes were a little faded, but we prayed. A family member contacted me and shared that they had heard Laura had died, years before. I thought it was impossible. Surely her husband would have told me. His parents would have contacted us. I searched with the little information given me and learned that she had committed suicide and had been cremated in a facility less than a mile away. Sadness covered me, and anger swept through me. Why not tell me, or my family? Laura's husband always wanted to be her protector and save her from her demons. Her therapist had refused to speak to me. I felt they each had betrayed me, keeping me from her, and now they had even cheated me out of saying goodbye.

Anger, bitterness, resentment, and depression were the result. I cried almost every day. I thought our family must have closure. We, our immediate family, had a service to say goodbye to bring about some closure. My sister-in-law made two collages of Laura. Her sisters suffered. We knew our hope of ever reuniting was now lost. Worse, we struggled with shame. Not knowing why she left, and not being able to help her haunted me. We struggled with anger, mostly toward her husband, for keeping us out of her life, and not telling us. It is the *Big Why*! Still unknown. Psalm 77:1–9 says:

> *I cried out to God to help; I cried out to God to hear me.*
> *When I was in distress, I sought the Lord;*
> *at night I stretched out untiring hands, and I would not be comforted.*
>
> *I remembered you, God, and I groaned; I meditated, and my spirit grew faint.*
> *You kept my eyes from closing; I was too troubled to speak.*
> *I thought about the former days, the years of long ago;*
> *I remembered my songs in the night. My heart meditated and my spirit asked:*
>
> *"Will the Lord reject forever? Will he never show his favor again?*
> *Has his unfailing love vanished forever? Has his promise failed for all time?*
> *Has God forgotten to be merciful? Has he in anger withheld his compassion?*

I struggled for years, praying that I could forgive and deal with the shame of Laura's death. I was working out the forgiveness of her husband, but the shame was more difficult. My wife, Jean, would say that the depression hanging over me lasted years. This had changed me. It was difficult to talk about Laura. I could only speak with Jean. Occasionally, I spoke with Bob and, sometimes, Jeanne. I prayed but experienced nothing. No light; only darkness.

God works in his own time. This suffering had made me more aware of other wounds buried deep within me. Bob and Jeanne had advised me to embrace the pain and not to avoid it. That was easier said than done for a person who had avoided anything that would disturb peace and tranquility as a life mission. The best I could do was cry almost every day. I rarely did this around anyone. I looked at Laura's pictures every day but rarely talked about her to anyone.

Three years passed. Then Faith, my youngest daughter, contacted us, and told us her family was going to celebrate Laura's birthday and asked if we would come. She had been telling her children about their Aunt Laura, and so the idea formed. Jean and I went to their house. Faith had purchased balloons. We said a few words, prayed, and then let some balloons go. We watched them disappear. The meaning was not lost. We had feelings of sadness and loss, and many tears, but we remembered her. She is not here, but she is not forgotten. A simple ceremony. A step. I had been in the darkness for some time, and now I had a little light. There was more ahead. I mourned. I prayed. *He* answered.

Sometime later, my friend Rick convinced me to go to a "Welcome Home Viet Nam Vets" celebration at the Maryland State Fairgrounds. I had served but spent the last 46 years avoiding dealing with my war experiences. I went and visited my friend, Allan, whose name was on the travelling Viet Nam Memorial: *The Wall.* I just "happened" to meet several Vets who washed *The Wall* every month. Bill, one of the vets, invited me to join the group. *The Wall,* as it has for many, became a place of healing for me but also a place where I could be involved in the healing of others. Now a small group of six men visit *The Wall* and meet the Viet Nam Vets from VVA 641. We have recognized, in a short ceremony at the end of washing, over 20 men whose names are on *The Wall* and whose families experienced the heartache of losing someone they love. I have been able to contact some of those family members to let them know we have not forgotten their loved one. In my pain, I have been able to comfort others, and the result has been healing for me. A step in helping to comfort others and, in turn, receiving God's comfort.

Faith did not stop with a birthday celebration. She invited Jean and me to an "Out of the Darkness Walk." Later, she directed a walk to benefit suicide prevention and asked us to volunteer. We remembered Laura and joined others who had suffered the loss of loved ones to suicide. My daughter, Kate, who lives in California, began doing walks and raising money for "Out of the Darkness" in Los Angeles.

Laura's suicide became easier to talk about. I am still careful. Many judgmental people do not understand and are insensitive with their comments about mental illness. I posted a few things about the walk and about Laura on her birthday. Many responded with support and, many who did not know how Laura had died, sent words of comfort. By bringing Laura's suicide into the light, I have received more comfort, and have been able to give comfort to others. Another step. Another Divine intervention.

> *Restore our fortunes, LORD, like streams in the Negev. Those who sow with tears will reap with songs of joy.*
> *Those who go out weeping, carrying seed to sow,*
> *will return with songs of joy, carrying sheaves with them* (Psalm. 126:4–6).

Shame will make you keep secrets. Shame will fester inside you, separating you from the people you love. Being more open and letting the light shine on this tragedy has enabled me to help others who have lost a child. Losing a child is a unique pain. You become part of a group no one wants to join. Just saying your child's name can cause pain. I have had tears come to my eyes and choked up many times while speaking about Laura or hearing others speak of their children. But God was not finished with me yet.

By going down to *The Wall*, my heart was being moved to help vets. A short time later, a friend of the family thought I might be interested in checking out a group at the Gilchrist Hospice. They were meeting to help, and to plan a "Welcome Home" celebration for Viet Nam Vets. I went through the volunteer program and got involved in recognizing vets though a "Salute to Service" ceremony for many who were in hospice care. Being with families who were experiencing this loss, and some who had already gone through it, has helped me see the importance of looking death in the face and empathizing with those who experience this pain. The men with whom I volunteer are a support to me and an example of love and comfort for those who are suffering. I waited. I prayed. God has answered and will continue to answer.

> *Praise be to the God and Father of our Lord Jesus Christ, the Father of compassion and the God of all comfort, who comforts us in all our troubles, so that we can comfort those in any trouble with the comfort we ourselves receive from God. For just as we share abundantly in the sufferings of Christ, so also our comfort abounds through Christ. If we are distressed, it is for your comfort and salvation; if we are comforted, it is for your comfort, which produces in you a patient endurance of the same sufferings we suffer. And our hope for you is firm, because we know that just as you share in our sufferings, so also you share in our comfort* (2 Corinthians 1:3–7).

God has brought me comfort through friends, family, and strangers who became friends. He has created good out of this tragedy. He keeps working in me although, at times, I am still trying to seek peace on my terms. Tears still come as I look at my favorite picture of Laura. I will always have a hole in my heart. I will always miss her as I wait for this temporary separation to end. At some point, my loss and pain will be completely healed. For now, I am rarely saddened by not being able to say goodbye. I have faced Laura's death: it is a temporary inconvenience. I know she loves me. I wait, and trust, for the time when we will embrace. For a time when, "There will be no more death or mourning or crying or pain." I wait. I pray, with hope and expectation, until we see each other again. The day we say, "Hello."

How I know Tim

I met Tim, while in college, when I was an atheist. He was very influential in helping me come to Christ. He has been one of my most faithful and trusted friends for over 40 years. He and his wife, Jean, both serve on the board of The Meadow and continue to support Jeanne and me in so many ways. The joy and laughter they bring into our lives is beyond words!

Where Healing Begins

What is rooted in the heart and mind controls a person. The heart is a small vessel filled with the good and bad of being human. It is filled with self-doubt, abandonment, and loathing but also with God and the treasure of grace and hope. Those who have suffered the loss of a love one or a close friend have suffered a deep wound in the heart. In the depths of our pain, the heart becomes the center for the transformation of our suffering. The movement from feeling abandoned travels to knowing that God is with us and for us. This helps us understand that we can realize a great purpose and hope in our suffering. The heart has unfathomable depths that transcend righteousness and wickedness. In it is death; in it is life.

During the ages of 17 to 23, I used drugs almost every day. Doing drugs helped me to deaden my inner struggles and allowed my mind to recklessly enter into an abyss. After becoming a Christian in my early 20s, I started to wonder about the meaning of Paul's admonition to "Take captive every thought" (2 Corinthians 10:5, NIV 1984). Wow, to think I could be in touch with every thought that came into my mind was beyond anything I could imagine. Originally, I assumed this verse meant to capture every thought intellectually. I thought the correct theology could make me healthy. Over time, however, I found that taking thoughts captive involved far more than dealing with mere intellectual ideas. It also involved emotions, woundedness, sorrow, and other thoughts and feelings.

The path to recovery and healing requires getting in touch with all the thoughts that affect us. These are the key ideas that lead to healing and recovery: *awareness, creating a safe place to examine my heart, and knowing the unconditional love and complete forgiveness of God.* Denying the thoughts that affect us can become an enemy to our heart and to our healing.

When Marcie died, I could have taken my thoughts of any given failure as a parent and let that give me a sense of shame. Instead, I became aware of those thoughts, and through the unconditional love and total forgiveness of God, I was able to overcome my feelings of shame. This became a path of peace and freedom, versus a path of self-loathing.

We must create safety in our hearts that allows us to accept the realities we don't want to admit but actually do exist. The foundation of finding our safety is knowing that God loves us unconditionally. He loves us for who we are, not for who we are supposed to be. He is madly in love with us! And because God loves us so much, he is willing to forgive us for all of our sins, past, present, and future. This creates a safe place, which leads us to an awareness and acknowledgement of all that is true about us. Accepting the truth, lets light enter into darkness, leading us to a path of freedom and healing. Becoming aware of the antagonism in our heart, a little at a time, and taking our thoughts captive, will allow the struggles within our heart to accept the love and forgiveness of Christ.

An old Cherokee told his grandson, "My son, a battle is raging between two wolves inside us all. One is evil. It is anger, jealousy, greed, resentment, inferiority, lies, and ego. The other is good. It is joy, peace, hope, love, humility, kindness, empathy, and truth."[xx]

The boy thought about it, and asked, "Grandfather, which wolf wins?"

The man quietly replied, "The one you feed."

Be Still, My Soul

(Katharina von Schlegal) 1750

'Still, mein Wille, dein Jesus hilft siegen"

The words of this song were magnificent words of comfort to me. Sometimes the only comfort we can have is to tell our souls to be still, and know the Lord is on our side.

Be still, my soul; the Lord is on thy side.
Bear patiently the cross of grief or pain.
Leave to thy God to order and provide.
In every change; He faithful will remain.
Be still, my soul: thy best, thy heavenly Friend
Through thorny ways leads to a joyful end.

Be still, my soul: thy God doth undertake
To guide the future, as He has the past.
Thy hope, thy confidence let nothing shake;
All now mysterious shall be bright at last.
Be still, my soul: the waves and winds still know
His voice Who ruled them while He dwelt below.

Be still, my soul: when dearest friends depart,
And all is darkened in the vale of tears,
Then shalt thou better know His love, His heart,
Who comes to soothe thy sorrow and thy fears.
Be still, my soul: thy Jesus can repay
From His own fullness all He takes away.

Be still, my soul: the hour is hastening on
When we shall be forever with the Lord.
When disappointment, grief and fear are gone,
Sorrow forgot, love's purest joys restored.
Be still, my soul: when change and tears are past
All safe and blessed we shall meet at last.

Be still, my soul: begin the song of praise
On earth, be leaving, to Thy Lord on high;
Acknowledge Him in all thy words and ways,
So shall He view thee with a well pleased eye.

Be still, my soul: the Sun of life divine
Through passing clouds shall but more brightly shine.

Silence

Nothing has helped me deal with my great sadness more than silence. Each morning when I wake up, I spend a great deal of time reading Scripture and being silent before the Lord. Slowing down is so important. As a result, I was able to take my thoughts captive, one at a time. Learning to be silent has helped me expose my fear, shame, and anger, and it removes their toxic noise. Being silent before the Lord has helped strengthen my mind and heart, making me more aware of my feelings. It has helped to strengthen my mind to stay in the present moment, away from useless distractions.

Henri Nouwen shared his experience: *"But when we enter into silence, we encounter a lot of inner noises, often so disturbing, that a busy and distracting life seems preferable to a time of silence"* ("Being Merciful with Ourselves," *Daily Email*, February 2).

Silence is one of the most misunderstood ideas in our world. It seems like a grand and romantic idea. This is often pictured as venturing into nature to capture the beauty, listen to the birds, and be surrounded by the quiet of creation. This romantic concept of silence quickly loses its zest. Nature does not silence our minds. Ants, mosquitoes, and flies are everywhere. The distracting noise in our head still dominates our thoughts. Even though these thoughts continue to return, we must be aware of their disruption.

No place is totally silent! But we should find a place of least distraction where we can meet with God without interruptions. *The key to silence is avoiding toxic noise.* We must quiet all unhealthy and harmful chatter.

When I consider silence, I realize that it is more complex than we might realize. We may think of "silence" as simply the absence of noise—quite passive. But it also involves choice and action. This means that learning to quiet the noise of our fear, shame, and anger, so we can enter the presence of God.

"'Be still and know that I am God,'" from Psalm 46:10 is mostly misunderstood. We think, if we just quiet ourselves and our surroundings, God will be fully present to us. When we try to get quiet, however, the noise will swell, and our minds will wander in every direction.

To be silent and present to God, we must learn how to

silence the noise. Psalm 46 is not telling us about "silence" as a passive noun. To the contrary, to experience true silence before God, we need to aggressively tell our many voices of noise to "be quiet."

Silence as a noun is a destination where we enter into God's presence. It is about knowing his compassion, that he is furiously in love with us, and that he desires his very best for us. It is about knowing the God of Mystery. It is about standing in awe before a God who is beyond our ability to understand. It is knowing that each moment, as big or little, as it may be, is God's moment for us to live in, to enjoy, and to be blessed. It is about making every moment sacred!

Silence is also a discipline, an exercise that helps create space for being "still" before God. The more we practice the discipline, the more the muscle of silence helps us get in touch with ourselves and how to enter the presence of God. Developing our spiritual muscles is achieved gradually, not overnight. We must, constantly, practice being silent to develop spiritual muscles of silence.

Silence reawakens the senses and becomes a way for us to learn. It helps us get in touch with our emotions, especially fear, shame, and anger. It strengthens our minds to be more aware of what we are thinking and feeling. We are able to become aware of what is happening to us in our minds; What are we sad about? Why are we depressed? Why are we feeling what we are feeling? I have found that practicing silence is a beneficial exercise to help me deal with sorrow and grief.

The Sacrament of the Present Moment

It is to be fully present, in the present moment, in the presence of the Holy Spirit.
God is fully present to us, and he desires that we would invite and accept his presence.

When you have experienced death's darkness and felt its sword pierce deep into your heart and soul, the pain is excruciating and beyond comprehension. I remember the second night after we had heard about Marcie's death, I was lying on a couch, not really sure I would survive the night. The darkness seemed impenetrable.

"How could I possibly live with this much pain?" I was now experiencing a new normal that had encountered deep sorrow and loss. To survive I had to learn to live in the present moment, to forgive and forget the past, and to not worry about the future.

Again and again, I needed to depend on the Psalms to find comfort in the darkest of darkness.

I cry aloud to the LORD; I lift up my voice to the LORD for mercy,
When my spirit grows faint within me, it is you who watch over my way.
Listen to my cry, for I am in desperate need;
rescue me from those who pursue me, (my past and future),
for they are too strong for me (Psalm 142:1, 3, 6).

Jean-Pierre de Caussade wrote a notable book—*The Sacrament of the Present Moment*— about finding God through total surrender and acceptance of everyday obstacles. The book explains that for us to live with peace of mind and rest for our souls, in this reality of death, loss, and sadness, we must, first, stay focused in the present moment. [xxi]

Through the years, I have learned that God is sufficient for this moment in time. In my mind and in my heart, I must remain fully present to him in the here and now. If I dwell on the past, I become quite vulnerable to shame. If I dwell on the future, I become vulnerable to dread and fear.

In his insightful book, *The Screwtape Letters* (chapter XV), C.

S. Lewis writes about how living in the past, present, and future affect us. He states that Satan is most effective when he succeeds at having us focus on the past and the future. Satan's weapons of fear, shame, and anger are very effective when we think about the future and the past. God, on the other hand, is most effective in our lives, as we live in the present moment.[xxii]

Fear, Shame, and Anger

The toxic noise of our souls are arrows of evil!

During each day, as we live with our sorrow, three arrows of evil constantly attack our heart. *These are fear, shame, and anger.* They each play an important role in disrupting our ability to face our sorrow and, ultimately, hinder our healing.

Fear primarily is an attack on our security in the future. Living in fear will controls many of our decisions as well as our ability to live fully and trust God for our lives.

Shame, for many, can be overwhelming, affecting one's identity, self-image. It leaves us with a deep sense of self-hatred and a belief that our life has no value. Its power hinders our ability to allow ourselves to be forgiven from our pasts, especially, our ability to be forgiven for how we have treated our loved ones.

Anger arises out of lack of control over our lives and the people in them. It strikes at our very souls and keeps us from being present to the love and forgiveness of God. When we surrender to God, we leave the toxic noise that tries to steal our path to peace.

All our struggles can be reduced to these three main toxic arrows. *Fear, shame, and anger* can clearly be traced back to the source of our worries and disruptions. Although everyone experiences a level of fear, shame, and anger, one of these emotions tends to rise to the surface in a person. Recognizing and acknowledging fear, shame, or anger in our lives as toxic noises that are   present will helps us released their grip. Most importantly, doing this will allow us to see what might be holding us back from dealing with our sorrow. We can find relief from the toxic lies of fear, shame, and anger by being still and silent in the presence of God.

The Future Never Exists; Only the Present

One night shortly after Marcie's death, I woke up in a state of fear. I became totally obsessed with the future and what life would be like without her. An intense time of prayer released me from this paralyzing fear. Looking back, my fear seems so irrational.

Throughout my years of teaching ministry classes, I have taught lessons about the past, present, and future. I have often challenged the audience to predict one thing that they think will happen in the future. Usually an awkward time of silence follows; then, after some reflection, most admit they cannot guarantee one thing that will happen. Next, I ask, if anyone can declare that they will be alive tomorrow or even later today. Again no one can make the guarantee.

The future is unknowable and beyond our control; yet we spend a great deal of time thinking and planning for it. We can even miss out on what is happening around us because we consume so much of today trying to plan for a safe tomorrow. In reality, most of what we worry about never happens.

Obsessing on future can evoke fear. How can we cope with a future over which we have no control? When will life bring another tragedy? Those who have lost a child can fear that we could lose another one.

This became painfully real to us when we learned that all our children suffered from the same heart defect that had led to Marcie's death. A dark cloud of fear surrounded us! Would another one of our children die just as Marcie had?

To think and imagine what life could be like in one, five, or ten years can be overwhelming. I can only survive when I stay focused in the moment. I must deal, only, with what I am facing right now. The pain is so great that if I let the fear of the future dominate my mind, I will be frustrated and depressed.

I, now, believe that Jesus' message is focused on the present. The present moment is the real reality of what Christ has done and will be doing in our lives. He tells us not to have anxiety and not to worry about the future. He tells us his strength will be sufficient then, as it is now. We must remember that today's problems are enough and adding to them the worries of tomorrow does no good. All our thoughts must run through

God's love and plans for us. Read Jesus' powerful words from The Sermon on the Mount:

> *"Therefore, I tell you, do not worry about your life, what you will eat or drink; or about your body, what you will wear. Is not life more than food, and the body more than clothes? Look at the birds of the air; they do not sow or reap or store away in barns, and yet your heavenly Father feeds them. Are you not much more valuable than they? Can any one of you by worrying add a single hour to your life?*

> *"And why do you worry about clothes? See how the flowers of the field grow. They do not labor or spin. Yet I tell you that not even Solomon in all his splendor was dressed like one of these. If that is how God clothes the grass of the field, which is here today and tomorrow is thrown into the fire, will he not much more clothe you— you of little faith? So do not worry, saying, 'What shall we eat?' or 'What shall we drink?' or 'What shall we wear?' For the pagans run after all these things, and your heavenly Father knows that you need them. But seek first his kingdom and his righteousness, and all these things will be given to you as well. Therefore do not worry about tomorrow, for tomorrow will worry about itself. Each day has enough trouble of its own"* (Matthew 6:25–34).

The Past, Our Shame, and Our Memories

The past, our shame and our memories can be loud, poisonous voices that increase the pain in our minds. They can tempt us into interrupting the sacrament of the present moment.

If I begin remembering the past, I can easily be overwhelmed by shame. I could have done so much for Marcie. I was not always the best parent. I was not always there for her. Marcie was an amazing gift. She was so wonderful, and our times together were so amazing, but now she is gone, and I am helpless to bring her back.

Somehow, we must accept the reality that the past is done. Its shame no longer exists. The past is gone, and mercy covers the feelings of shame.

One night, as I was sitting in the depth of depression, I began to think of Marcie and her life in heaven and wondering what she was thinking about me. In her new existence, I realized that to her, none of the failures of our past had any meaning. She had been forgiven for all of her sins, and she had totally forgiven us of ours. Her failure and shame of the past was no longer a reality. And now, her hope for us was to move into the next journey of our life, knowing fully that all is well with Marcie. She, right then, only desired the best for us!

To dwell on the past can be dangerous. When I do, I begin to be tempted by feelings of failure and shame over what I have done or have failed to do. I need to stay focused in the present. Marcie is now living in an incredible, beautiful, awesome, new reality. For us, God is fully present—an ever-present hope—and has a new journey for us. Our shame from the past is forgiven. Saint John of the Cross warns us to be very careful when we begin dwelling on the past (Iain Matthew, *The Impact of God*[xxiii], pp.105–106). Often, thoughts of the past can fill us with guilt and shame. Examine your own thoughts of the past and see if what I am saying is true.

The part of the past that we must believe is God's faithfulness to us. Scripture exhorts us to remember his faithfulness, especially in his deliverance of the Jewish people from their slavery in Egypt (see, for example, Psalm 103:7–18; John 4:14–17; Acts 7:36–41; Hebrews 3:15–19).

The healing of our memories is a vital link to the depths of our pain and suffering. Some memories come with a deep woundedness that can still play an intrusive role in our lives. God may heal some of those memories without us even knowing. With some memories in our suffering, however, we need to seek times of silent contemplation in order to bring about our healing.

Faith, Hope and Love

First of all, my child, think magnificently of God.
Magnify His providence; adore His power.
Pray to Him frequently and incessantly. Bear Him always in your
mind.
Teach your thoughts to reverence Him in every place;
for there is no place where He is not.
Therefore, my child, fear and worship and love God;
first and last, think magnificently of Him!
"Advice to a Son"—Paternus

Faith, hope, and love are the great theological virtues. They are what remain; with love being the greatest (1 Corinthians 13:13). They are the eyes of our heart. They function in the unseen world and become a foundation of transformation as we enter into suffering.

Remember back to the advice of the Cherokee grandfather to his grandson? Our minds hold the struggle in our hearts between good and evil. They must be fed to survive. Whichever we feed, will survive, so we must feed the good to be filled with good. Choosing the virtues of faith, hope, and love gives us the foundation to fight against the voices that want to destroy us and fill us with despair. We must live in the present moment and not let the future or the past dominate our lives. Do not feed your heart with fear, shame, or anger but free your heart with the truths of faith, hope, and love.

Faith, hope, and love allow us to see God as love. We can see him, personally, involved with every one of the seven billion people on earth. He is deeply involved with our suffering because our wounds are his wounds, and our suffering was, first, his suffering.

In his excellent book, *The Impact of God,* Fr. Iain Matthew, rightly proposes God's idea of faith, hope, and love expressed together: "*But where God is concerned, the problem lies in our desiring too little, and growing means expanding our expectations, or rather making his generosity, not our poverty the measure of our expectation. We see in God, a lavish God and we can believe in a God whose power is beyond anything I know and believe in a God whose love is unlike any that we know, and believe in Christ who is an unfathomable mine, with seam after seam of treasury"*[xxiv].

This magnified view of God gives us power to overcome the forces of evil in the battlefield of the heart. We know, with certainty, that God desires to bring goodness into our life, and he is with us and for us!

Faith

When we experience the kind of suffering we are highlighting in this book, we may be led to believe that God doesn't love us and that in our suffering we are getting what we deserve. This is, essentially, what Job's accusers told him. Just the opposite is true!

We fear what other people think. We fear what the future may bring. We worry about money and our possessions. Instead of living before the audience of thousands, we need to learn to live before the audience of One!

Faith is believing who God is. Ultimately, faith is best understood as trust. When we walk into our dark places where little is recognizable, we must rely on faith. We may not know where we are going or what tomorrow will bring, but we can trust in a God who knows where he wants us to go. And, because of his great power and love, we can rest in the day, knowing that he holds our future in his hands.

God's strength and goodness can carry us, no matter what our situation. As Julian of Norwich wrote in her book, *Showings*, "All shall be well, and all shall be well, and, all manner of things, shall be well" (p. 225).

The God we know entered into the world as a human being and suffered all that we have suffered. The empty cross symbolizes Christ's death, resurrection, and empty grave. His wounds, suffering, and death hold the power for us to live in the midst of our deepest suffering. Jesus' resurrection from death gives us a vision and the power to live beyond the life we now have. *"Now faith is confidence in what we hope for and assurance of what we do not see"* (Hebrews 11:1).

Hope

Hope believes that God will do what he promised. It is the virtue of expectation. Hope knows that God is good and that he forgives us. God cleanses us and desires to make us beautiful. He wants to enrich and enlighten us.

Where God is concerned, hope attains as much as it hopes for. Our view of God either limits or expands what God actually desires to do for us. Hope is a refusal to let our memories or the world determine who we are. Our hope should be in God and what wants for us.

Love

Love desires what God desires. Love is not the essence of every virtue but the essential motive behind them. Love is a gift by which we choose God and all he desires and wills. Through love, we align our wills to God's perfect will. Pure and simple: it is our surrender to him by letting God and letting go!

Understand that *love* means desiring what God desires is a breakthrough idea. Why wouldn't we desire what God desires? He is good. He is perfect in his *love* for us. He wants to bring his very best into our lives. Clearly, for ourselves, and for others, we should desire what God desires.

And regarding *love* between individuals, our goal in loving should be to desire the very best for others. First Corinthians 13:4–8) describes *love*. A helpful practice is to insert God's name in place of the word "love."

> God is patient,
> God is kind.
> God does not envy,
> God does not boast,
> God is not proud.
> God does not dishonor others,
> God is not self-seeking,
> God is not easily angered,
> God keeps no record of wrongs.
> God does not delight in evil but rejoices with the truth.
> God always protects, always trusts, always hopes, always perseveres.
> God never fails!

Getting Personal

One of the most neglected group people in the grieving process are families who have suffered miscarriages, especially the women who had been pregnant. For some reason, our culture does not recognize the grieving of a woman who has lost a child. After enduring the miscarriage, she is expected to move on as though nothing has happened. Miscarriage, however, is a very difficult and emotionally painful experience for the woman who has carried a baby and then must face the reality of a lost child.

In the last few years, a good friend of mine suffered a miscarriage near the end of her pregnancy. Knowing her pain made me acutely aware of the depth of suffering that a family, especially the woman, has to face.

This family put together a grieving process that honored the baby and acknowledged their loss. When they learned their preborn baby had died, they decided to wait until the birth occurred naturally. Thus, they mourned together and waited 18 hours for the birth of their child.

Then they put together a funeral service and burial ceremony. More than 100 people attended the beautiful service.

In the process, we learned that many of the women in the audience had experienced miscarriages, with most never having had a time to process their grief.

John and Tee Kelly's story of the loss of Faith describes the beautiful and awesome process of how they mourned the death of their child.

Faith Rises

by Tee and John Kelly

My husband, John, was in a finalist presentation when he got the call. He let the meeting participants know that his wife was about to have a baby and that this could be "go time."

Earlier that day, I had gathered up our four children—Hannah, eight; Johnny, six; Allie, four; Lydia, two—to go for our last appointment before the delivery of our daughter.

We had named her Faith Marguerite at 18 weeks when we learned she was a girl: Marguerite after John's mom and Faith out of a sense of God's leading. We tried to name all our children with a sense of meaning and out of God's leading, believing that a part of our identity emerges in our name. We felt like we knew Faith already, having spent unusual amounts of time talking to her, singing to her, and watching her move around in my womb. As our living faith must be, our daughter Faith was active in my womb.

My appointment that day, July 27, 2000, seemed like all our prior appointments: our children were usually in the room with me as the miracle of life, her life, was shown on the sonogram screen. Dr. Aziz had always been there, but on this day as I was lying on the table, I learned she had an emergency over at the hospital and that our nurse, Denise, would be caring for me. As she moved the wand around on my stomach, she asked a question she had not asked before, "Have you felt the baby move?" I said I had but was not sure when the last time was that I had felt her move. Each of our children moved closer to push on my belly to see if she would kick.

When Denise told me I would need to go over to the hospital to have them take a look, I collected my belongings, our four children, and began walking towards the bridge to the hospital. I am not inclined to think the worst, so in my mind I figured the sonogram machine must not have been working properly because Dr. Aziz wasn't there. On my way over I felt a little confused as to where I was going. As we passed my pediatrician's office, I stopped to ask for directions. Dolores quickly offered a helping hand. I told her where I was headed and that I wasn't sure how to get there. She picked up on the potential reality looming and asked if I wanted her to contact John. I said, "No, let me figure out what's going on first." She immediately offered to come with me and wait with the children in the waiting room. I had a slight thought in my mind that something wasn't right, but my more prominent thought was, "That would never happen to me." When the attending doctor at the hospital informed me, with compassion and sadness, that there was no heartbeat, I sat there in complete shock. The tears started to flow, but it still felt so surreal and impossible.

The doctor left the room; and I called John on his cell phone; but because he was in a meeting, he did not answer. The next call went to the receptionist at the client's office, who interrupted the meeting to get John. John excused himself. When I told him, "They couldn't find a heartbeat, she's dead," I could feel his emotions rising in his initial moment of pain and sorrow to meet me in mine and the disbelief in what he was hearing. John remembers the exact place and moment he was told. He, too, didn't want to believe what he had just heard. His associate, Mark, had driven that day, so John brought Mark up interstate 95, himself in silence, as John wept. It was a long ride for John, and he has spoken often of the tears, the array of emotions, and the pain of being unable to help us all carry this reality together.

I was so grateful that our children were with me. Their presence was such a comfort to me as we waited for John to arrive. When John walked in, we clung to each other as the reality of this loss began to sink in—we would never look into the eyes of our daughter, ad she would never grasp the hands of her siblings. As followers of Jesus, we also began to wonder how the blessedness and comfort promised by Jesus in the Sermon on the Mount would be made real. These were painful moments and only the beginning of a mourning that would work in peculiar ways, noting that even the early moments of confusion and denial proved to be a part of God's gentle hand.

As the reality of important decisions loomed, Dr. Aziz arrived, her presence a comfort as well, to tell us I had to deliver Faith and that she had to go away the next morning. I could not imagine delivering a full term still born child, and I needed Dr. Aziz's caring compassionate presence to help me through. We prayed for a speedy delivery.

My parents (who lived five hours away) were on their way to meetings in Washington D.C. and immediately diverted their trip to arrive at the hospital within an hour of hearing the news. John's parents and brothers arrived quickly as well. My sisters and brother left their responsibilities on our farm in Western Pennsylvania to arrive before the delivery. The presence of family and friends felt like the hands and feet of God himself. In times like this, words are insufficient, so they mostly sat in silence. I was able to deliver Faith before Dr. Aziz had to leave, as her tender hands were the first to touch all our children, and her presence gave me strength I needed.

It is hard to describe the depths of our grief when we first saw her and held her. She was so precious. Eight and a half pounds, twenty-two and half inches long, she looked like a beautiful, peaceful, sleeping baby. She looked like Allie. The pain was so deep, as if our hearts were literally being broken in two. I had not realized how much we loved this child whom we had not yet seen or touched. This deep sense of loss awakened me to the depth of connection a mother has with her children as they are formed and developed in her womb. Part of how we mourned involved a decision we made to hold her and touch her and let our family do the same. Our children came in first and were able to deeply connect to their sister and put reality around the array of emotions they were experiencing. Our parents held her; our brothers and sisters held her. Each time a new family member arrived the nurses would bring Faith back to us wrapped up in a blanket and looking so precious.

St. Joseph's is a Catholic hospital, one that values life in all its stages, and they were all so wonderful in comforting us as we delivered our stillborn child in the maternity ward filled with mothers bringing their living children into the world. We wondered how each new shift nurse or doctor was so aware of our loss and treated us with such tender care and comfort. When we left the hospital, we noticed on the placard outside our door they had inserted a picture of a falling leaf to signify we had lost our child. We still have that little card.

As hours turned into days, more decisions had to be made. We began thinking of how to honor Faith's life. We decided to have a memorial service. John wanted to honor her life in this way, and he wanted us each to eulogize her. I could not imagine doing this, and I told him I did not think I could. Then I went to take a shower; and as the water beat down, I sensed the warmth of the Spirit of the Lord giving me words to express our love for Faith, for one another, and for his love and faithfulness in the midst of our deep sorrow. I came out and wrote down, in 10 minutes, what the Lord had given me. I was able to eulogize her at the memorial, and I am so thankful we had the funeral and that we were able to honor her life.

John and I have learned that we mourn differently. John's words for the service came to him during very raw questioning of God: "Why Lord? Why did you allow this?" The Lord led John so beautifully, strengthening and comforting him, and giving him the words to share at the service and, later, deep insights into the questions he continued to ponder. We have learned afresh through this and the many challenges of this life, that faith is a gift, a promised seed, an active, rising source of strength. As the apostle Paul learned, this life we live, we live by faith, the very "faith of" the son of God who gave himself for us (Galatians 2:20. KJV).

Our pastor at the time, Chuck Faber, led the memorial service. Chuck was such a good friend, tenderly loving and serving us. He helped us put the program together as we chose the songs and Scriptures. My grandmother read a poem that she wrote, integrating her faith and the short life of her great granddaughter, Faith. Our mothers each read from the Scriptures, and our fathers were the pallbearers. We had an open casket, and Faith lay there like a beautiful sleeping baby as we received more than 400 people. It meant the world to us that so many came to share in our grief and to honor Faith's short life. The songs we sang are forever dear to us: "Be Still, My Soul," "Savior, Like a Shepherd Lead Us," "I Lift Up My Eyes," "Faithful God" and "Jesus Loves Me." The third stanza of "Be Still, My Soul" especially ministered to me because it was just what God did in our lives. It says,

> *Be still, my soul, when dearest friends depart, and all is darkened in the veil of tears. Then shalt thou better know His love, His heart, who comes to soothe thy sorrow and thy fears."*

John spoke about his dream of walking Faith down the aisle someday and giving her away to a loving husband. Tears flowed as he went on to share how the Lord had spoken to him, reminding him that the bridegroom was present and that we were indeed giving our daughter away that day to her bridegroom and ours, Christ Jesus our

Lord.

For seven days, visitors came to our home, bringing meals and flowers, sitting with us, and comforting us. Our Jewish brothers and sisters have it so right in the concept of sitting Shiva. Something is so powerful about presence, not trying to have answers but just being near. Over time, people would share stories and send letters describing how they had been affected by Faith's memorial service. Some shared about giving their life to Jesus, others about rededicating themselves to trust and follow him. One couple felt compelled to get rid of their TV for a season. Clearly the Holy Spirit did this, as all we wanted to do was honor our daughter's life and God's nearness in our sorrow.

We were so thankful at how God led us through these early days. Eventually, though, it was just us again—me, John, Hannah, Johnny, Allie, and Lydia, all trying to work through our own sense of loss. Our oldest daughter, Hannah, had prepared Faith's clothes and room and would sit alone in that space. Johnny told us that Jesus could raise her from the dead, like He did Lazarus. Allie released a balloon one day for her and watched it go up in the sky, declaring, "I wonder if that balloon will reach heaven where God, Jesus, and Faith will see it?" Lydia would pat my tummy when someone visited and declare emphatically, "Faith died. She is in heaven with God and Jesus."

We are 20 years removed from Faith's passing and have come to realize that mourning is like the waves of the sea. In the storm, during the early days, the waves come hard and fast; but even when the sun returns and the winds calm, they still roll in, albeit gently and softly. Living life here, knowing we have a daughter on the other side, keeps us mindful that heaven is just a veil away. We visit her grave annually, sing the songs together from her funeral, lay stones to remember her, and thank God for his faithfulness.

For each of our children, on their first birthday, John would go away alone and write a poem for them. These poems, all these years later, have proven to have prophetic meaning and insights only God could have given him when he wrote them. On July 28th, the day after Faith passed, John went away alone and wrote a poem for her. This poem also has prophetic meaning and is a source of strength for us, even today. We included it in the memorial service program.

Faith Marguerite

Faith, the substance of things hoped for.
The evidence of things not seen.
Faith,
The child you've taken home
The gift that comes from Your throne.

And gifts You give Lord,
Are always good,
Tho sometimes in this place,
They cannot be understood.

So here we live,
In this place filled with tears,
While our precious child, Faith
Lives where there are no fears.

Give us strength, Oh God,
To walk this road,
This narrow path You lead us on.
Your Light, the glory, of a coming dawn.

For you will return,
To take us home.
Where we, like Faith
Will rest beneath Your throne.

And see again,
This child You've taken.
With You at our side,
We will not be shaken.

Love, your dad (July 28, 2000)

We, indeed, have experienced God at our side, though the process of mourning never fully ceases. For a while, we struggled with how God could have let this happen, even at times blaming God. Chuck shared a story at the funeral about how a shepherd leads his stubborn sheep to higher ground as the heat of summer looms. He explained that a good shepherd knows what is best for his sheep and, if necessary, will take a baby ewe, break her leg, lay her on his shoulders, and began to walk the narrow mountain path upward. The mothers would begin to follow, and soon the rest of the sheep would follow as well. Eventually, he shared, they would all reach the higher ground where food and water were available, and comfort was found. In that moment, we trusted that our little child was on the Good Shepherd's shoulders and being carried to higher ground. John and I committed to remembering the thin veil between the reality of our loss and the promise of eternal gain and comfort for Faith and for us when our time in this present reality is finished. King David said, when he lost his son, "I will go to him, but he will not return to me" (2 Samuel 12:22). We still mourn, but it is more like gentle waves. We still ask questions; we still seek God; and we know now more than ever that God raised Faith from the dead and that he continues to give us the faith we need to walk the narrow path he leads us on.

By God's grace we brought two more children into the world since Faith's passing, our two youngest sons, Micaiah and Boaz. We remember well how tired we were when Faith was conceived, and how sorrowful we were when she passed. I am not sure we would have chosen to have two more children after Faith, but we knew our family wasn't complete after she died. Today Mic and Bo join us in remembering their sister, and we see these two boys as living reminders of the life that often comes through loss. For through difficult challenges indeed, "Faith Rises."

How I Know John & Tee

They are wonderful friends that I first met in the 90s. John and I have done men's ministry together for years. They've hosted many Meadow events in their home as well as being great supporters to Jeanne and me. John and Tee's story of losing their daughter had a powerful impact on us and also on our church community, Grace Fellowship Church in Timonium, MD.

Our Sacred Moments

Death Encountered and Life Awakens

My life was filled with a newfound strength when I awakened to the reality of death. The great paradox of the aftermath of Marcie's death and the devastation that it brought into our lives was such that we would have never wanted to live our lives having missed it. In no way, of course, would we have wanted our daughter to die; however, in no way would we want to have missed the movement of God in our lives afterwards.

The most terrible moment of our life turned into a gift. Those who have experienced the death of a child may well have been given a great gift.

The gift left by the death of a child, partner, parent, brother, sister, colleague, or friend, always leads to a heightened awareness of life. We become more aware of life; thus we are able to experience our delight in commonplace, everyday life.

A few months after Marcie's death, I completed my first journal with these words:

> *I am finishing one of the most crucial journals of my life. Even as I complete it, in my mind, I am walking a pilgrimage through the events of the past months with a deep wound. Along with it, I have a deep desire to heal that wound, or at least find out how to live with it. It has been an intense four months, full of sadness and sorrow. Yet, it has been a time when I have met God in ways beyond what I thought possible. This I will always cherish. I would never want to return to "normal" or to what life was before.*
>
> *The spike that has wounded my soul has placed itself deeply into the soil, and, well planted, it continues to produce a harvest of righteousness. I do not know where it is leading, but it is leading me.*
>
> *Somewhere I read a statement by a wife, who was living through the death of her husband, "I know that this is a sacred time, and I must record its events to remember God in the midst of this sacred time."*
>
> *Surely, for us to walk through the devastation of death leads us into a "Dark Night of the Soul," a poem written by John of the Cross. The "dark night" may simply refer to an experience of loss and desolation. In Spanish, the title reads, "The Obscure Night of the*

Soul." It is obscure because it is a deep encounter with God, which is difficult to understand and put into words. When we encounter God, the real God, face to face, it is like being in a deep forest or the ocean or a white-out in winter. God is so great, so amazing, so beyond our finite abilities, that his presence is overwhelming. We have no recognition of grace or liberation in our darkness. If gratitude is felt, it is simply for having survived. At other times, we have a strong sense that the experience, however unpleasant or pleasant, was a catalyst for being open to receive the gift of grace.

There can be a reason to offer thanksgiving for having had the experience; even though one might never want to repeat it. As, I'm sure, others have felt, I feel this way about many of life's experiences. The dark night's transformative nature, when it occurs with the death of a loved one, is very much like this. Over and over, we hear of people who have lost their love ones coming to recognize that the experience was a very sacred moment in their lives.

We wouldn't have missed it for the world, but we certainly would never want to go through it again. In our deepest sorrow and despair, God came to us in very unfamiliar, yet astounding ways!

Healing of Memories

God promises to bring a substantial psychological healing into our lives. This includes our sorrow and past and present woundedness from strongholds in our families.

Strongholds are walls that we put in our minds to help us cope with life. They can result from a deep wound or devastating encounter with life or something very small. When Jeanne was living in the Philippines, she told her uncle who was a doctor that she wanted to be a doctor when she grew up. He replied, "Oh no you can't be a doctor, only be a nurse.," creating a "stronghold, of sorts in her mind. It could be caused by something that our parents said to us or bullying we received in middle school. Strongholds become protective shields that run deep in our personality. They negatively affect us because they hold us back from experiencing all of life.

Through time, I became very aware that I lived in a constant state of fear. I was afraid of everything and wasn't sure why. As I became more and more familiar with contemplative prayer and learning to be silent in God's presence, I was led to begin exploring why I was so fearful.

Contemplative prayer is quite effective in bringing healing to our memories. It can help us explore the past and give us insight into what happened, which we might not have learned otherwise. Often, time is needed for the exploration and healing to occur.

Where did my fear originate? When exploring my past through contemplative prayer, I began to examine the source of my fears. The first recognition came when I realized that my mother was a fearful person. She processed all of life, especially her future, by lowering her expectations. Out of fear, she created the worst possible ending. Surely, this was the beginning of understanding my own fear.

Then within a few months, I asked the question: *Where did my mother's fear come from?* Somewhere I had heard that, in order to understand your family's strongholds, a good idea is to look at the stories in their history. One of the big events that occurred in my family was facing bankruptcy in the 1930s. My grandparents were living on a farm and were not able to meet their expenses, partly because they gave away milk to people in need who could not afford it.

While in prayer, I was led to consider the question, *How did my mother and her family feel the last day on the farm as they walked away from their land?* The despair and sorrow must have been overwhelming. I am certain my mother processed the rest of her life through this dreadful event. If that could happen in her past, it might occur again in her life. Eventually, my mother's deep fear was passed onto me. But the story does not end there.

God remembers our pain and returns to heal it. The book of Ruth has a wonderful story about the life of Naomi that illustrates this principle. Naomi had lost her sons as well as her husband. This was one of the most devastating things that could happen in the life of a woman in biblical times. Having no husband or son placed a woman in a vulnerable position in that culture. Men (and their role in society) provided women financial security and their essential identity.

Naomi went into a deep depression; even changing her name from Naomi to Mara, which means bitter. Her son's wife, Ruth, chose to stand with her, assuring her that, "Where you go, I will go, and where you stay, I will stay. Your people will be my people and your God my God. Where you die, I will die, and there I will be buried" (Ruth 1:16–17). Then they returned to Bethlehem together. The short of the story is that Ruth re-married and had a son. At the end of the story, we find Naomi holding Ruth's son and the women of the community declaring, "Naomi has a son!" (Ruth 4:17) Ruth's son was like a monument that stood over Naomi's life. God had remembered Naomi and made up for her loss. This son would become the father of Jesse, the father of David, the royal ancestor of Jesus! God remembered Nomi's pain and healed her.

God also came into my life to heal a life that filled with fear. Here is one of the most amazing statements that I have ever heard. My friend, Ann, from high school said, "I think God is leading me to give you 'The Benny'!" The Benny is a beautiful 67-acre farm that has two homes and is located in one of the most isolated parts of Western Maryland. We could hardly believe this amazing gift from such a generous friend. Eventually we changed its name from "The Benny" to "Marcie's Meadow."

The farm is filled with beauty. The early 1800s farmhouse

overlooks a wheat kissed meadow circled by beautiful wildflowers. The drive of the path takes you back in time, a simpler time. It sits nestled in a river valley near the calm waters of the Potomac. The second home is above the tree line and sits on the side of the mountain surrounded by lush trees and vegetation. this place is filled with natural beauty and rustic tranquility.

We could never have imagined how Ann's generosity and the land's beauty would contribute to a major part of our healing. The farm has become a place where we can rest and enjoy solitude. It is a land which yields to contemplation and meditation where God restores our souls. It also has become a place of community where families and friends can grow together and create memories, forming a fabric that binds us to Christ and his Kingdom. It has also become a cornerstone for our ministry where we have been able to host and share this amazing land with others. Mysteriously, by God's grace and through Ann's generous gift of part of her beautiful farm, it has become a monument that continually reminds me of God's healing of my fear. The stronghold has been broken. Marcie's Meadow has become a great place for our family's healing, and for all who visit.

After a few years at the farm, I came to a surprising observation. I realized that the farm was close to the same land that my mother's family had lost so many years ago. Interestingly, my sister, brother, and two of my nephews have properties located nearby on the Potomac or its tributaries. I clearly saw God remembering the deep pain in my mother's family history from 70 years ago, and now he had healed that familial pain. This monument reminds me of God's faithfulness.

Marcie's Meadow and the original farmhouse from the early 1800s in Western Maryland

Getting Personal

Sometimes the more difficult grieving occurs when it must be endured for a long time. Marcie's death happened in a matter of minutes, but for some the fight to live goes on for years.

Stuart and Tom Sweitzer had to live with Matthew's battle with cancer for over five years. Living this day in and day out, with the rest of life's struggles, can be overwhelming. Surely God's grace is essential to survive such an ordeal.

Yet Stuart was able to allow God to open to a bigger picture. "Our family was blessed with six kids, a home, friends, and so much more. . . . My question—Why not us?—came as I sat in our fifteen-passenger van nursing my little baby and people-watching outside the hospital. My next thought was that we were no better, no different, than the people I was watching. It was in that moment that my perspective changed. I prayed that God would give me the strength to not only get through my journey but that he would be right beside me in my journey using me to encourage and love others that he would put in my path."

Someone has said that in a war, Christians know how to fight. (They also know how to fight when in peacetime). Fred Rogers reminds us that when suffering occurs, we see the heroes arise. We can see how Stuart and Tom's friends rallied around them and supported them in their time of crisis.

Made to Love
by Stuart Sweitzer

This fall has been a whirlwind! As the excitement and anticipation of Thanksgiving approached this week, I purposefully spent time pondering things I was thankful for. I used the mega-hours spent driving, moments in the kitchen (when I was actually alone while the rest of the gang was involved in other hustle and bustle around the house), and lovely time outside raking and walking the dogs and gathering chicken eggs to think of many things for which I was thankful.

Not only is my list unending, but I am once again reminded of some things. Concentrating on the *good* helps to put pretty much *everything* in perspective. It helps to keep the "harder to deal with" things in life less pressing and has once again helped me see that although the media so consistently concentrates on the bad and the negative situations and people, a lot of good and caring people are out there.

The first time that I consciously thought about the reality of so many good, loving, and caring people, was a few months after my sixth child came into this world. He was born with cancer. Life for our family turned upside down. All that we knew changed in so many ways, and my heart was heavy and hurting. I hurt for my little baby and all he was enduring with surgeries, hospital visits, chemo, infections, and just feeling yucky. I ached for my children at home who were homeschooled and used to me being home all the time ... teaching, cooking, playing, hiking, going on fun day trips, etc. With our new life, they often woke up in the morning to find that in the middle of the night, the baby and I had left again to go to Johns Hopkins Hospital for days or even weeks. I worried about my marriage. I was running on autopilot and just knew that, statistically, many marriages did not survive when a child was critically ill.

So as life continued, because it just does, I kept having people ask me, "How this could happen to your family?" But one day, as I really noticed many others suffering, scared, and seeming so lost, I asked God, "Why not us?" My eyes were opened to see a bigger picture. Our family was blessed with six kids, a home, friends, and so much more. My question—Why not us?—came as I sat in our fifteen-passenger van nursing my little baby and people-watching outside the hospital. My next thought was that we were no better, no different, than the people I was watching.

In that moment, my perspective changed. I asked God to give me strength to not only get through the new journey we were on but to be right by my side and use me to encourage and love others that he would put in my path. I had a tough couple of years—five years really—but the first two were the most intense. My son was, and is, my hero. He turned seventeen this year!

I would not want to go through that again. But I am so thankful for so much during that time. We developed a new normal, and life went on. But amazing people made it bearable and even good, some of the time. We had strangers calling, bringing gifts, meals, and notes of encouragement. Friends stepped in and took care of arranging meals for the family at home when we left unexpectedly for Camp Hopkins for days or weeks at a time, pretty much each month. Fellow homeschoolers stepped in to help in so many ways. We had the best neighbors ever! My mom came to visit every time we were admitted. My sister moved in to help while carrying a full load of college work. We had such caring and loving nurses, doctors, Child Life specialists, and social workers! We met such sweet families who were roommates at the hospital, sometimes in the little kitchen when we just needed a break or when we wheeled our kids around the halls in little cars with one hand, while pushing IV poles with the other.

So, what I experienced during that time opened my eyes to the goodness in people. And this week as I considered my Thanksgiving list, I had to affirm that I am so thankful for the "best of the best"—the people in my life. The other stuff is nice, but it's just stuff. As I wrap up, I am thankful for this blog, *Made to Love*. That's why we are here: to love God and to not look at the people who we see on the news as just grim statistics but as real people with real stories.

How I know Stuart

I met Stuart (Stu) while running a Campus Life Club at the high school where she attended. Stuart would tell her parents that she was coming to club when she was actually hanging out with her friends and doing the foolish things that teenagers do. She was an amazingly bright kid with an adventurous side. She grew up to be a loving and compassionate mother. We have been friends since those early days which has continued for over 40 years. She and her wonderful husband, Tom, are great followers of Christ and serve many young people in the area today.

PART V
A Call to the Future

Introduction to Part V
A Call to the Future

All this is for your benefit, so that the grace that is reaching more and more people may cause thanksgiving to overflow to the glory of God (2 Corinthians 4:15).

A.W. Tozer said, "It is doubtful whether God can bless a man greatly, until he has hurt him deeply"[xxv] (*The Roots of the Righteous*, p. 165). Through our journey, God has allowed us to suffer greatly, and the suffering has prepared us to serve and join him to expand his kingdom. We all, at some point, will travel a path of sorrow, and we all will have the choice whether or not to experience our suffering in his presence. Through God's love, which we can come to know with certainty for ourselves, we have the opportunity to stretch out God's arms and extend his grace, love, peace, and compassion to others.

As a result of Marcie's death, we have learned the importance of making every second count and remaining focused on the present moment. We experience great joy when we see God using Marcie's life-story to influence her friends. We continue to see her impact, even today.

Moving forward after Marcie's death was difficult, but we have learned so much. The Meadow Ministry that we started was the beginning of a new chapter for us. Our desire has intensified to continue equipping those who hunger for a richer experience with Christ. We hope to bring faith, hope, and love to many and continue to encourage those who are going through life's suffering and sorrow.

As you walk through your own pain, I hope you will be able to discover your calling.

"Grief never ends... but it changes. It's a passage, not a place to stay. Grief is not a sign of weakness, nor a lack of faith. ... It is the price of love." Anonymous

Make Every Second Count

"Remembering may be a celebration; or it may be a dagger in the heart, but it is better, far better, than forgetting."—Donald M. Murray (*The Lively Shadow*, p.193)

Two and a half years have passed since Marcie died. What was once a very warm winter has become very cold, depressing, and lonely. I have lost my will to live. This morning I wake up and get out of bed, only because I can't sleep any longer. I don't feel like taking on the challenges of life.

I begin reading *A Lively Shadow* [xxvi] by Donald Murray. He wrote this book several years after his daughter had died at the age of 20 from Reye's Syndrome. Murry is not religious, so reading how he coped with his daughter's death is very depressing. But the reading brings me closer to Marcie's death and the whole experience around it. There is much to which I can relate.

After Murray's daughter died, he was very sullen. He wanted to be left alone, but people continued to invade his space. Later he realized that the intrusion he felt was good. I think back to the time during the funeral where much of my time was spent comforting others. Some had attended with apprehension, perhaps, sensing a remote fear that one day they might struggle with the same dreadful fate we were facing. Still, I was comforted by their presence. The person whose loved one has died and those who have come to offer comfort to the ones who are mourning engage in sort of a dance of comfort.

The message from Murray's book and the memories of my contacts at the funeral help remind me of how vitally precious every moment was that we had with Marcie.

We could say we took full advantage of our time with her, but, sadly, I would say that it wasn't nearly enough. If we could do it over, I would have done so much more.

Yesterday, I read in the *Cumberland Times-News*, of the death of one of my cousins. I had not seen him for over 30 years. He was one of my heroes when I was young and one of my father's favorites. They would spend time sharing drinks and conversations that would seem to go on for hours. I remember that my father never spent that kind of time with me.

I think back to the conversation I had with Marcie and Robert when they were preschool age. They wanted to learn about my father. I told them that he had died when I was 18 and that I had little or no involvement with him. Later, when they were older, in another conversation I told them that he never attended any of my sports activities. They were startled. In 26 years of parenting, I had missed very few of my children's games; probably less than ten. For me, every game was an exciting and wonderful event.

How I wish Marcie could, again, be a part of our life! If only she could see our new farm, *The Meadow*, and see Vee and Julie playing volleyball and Robert skeet shooting and be with us at Christmas. If, just one more time, we could walk on Holden Beach, and talk. Oh, how sad!

I realize that I am far from being over the loss of Marcie. Even now, frankly, every day, I think about her and mourn her loss. It still hurts very much. We are a family that will always be marked by the fact that one of our children is missing. We are a part of a fraternity of people who quietly mourn death yet have to continue to live as if it didn't happen.

Life is a series of opportunities. We never know how long we have to take advantage of them. Tomorrow, maybe even today, death could change everything around us. People who come to the funeral home to comfort those in mourning, especially after a child dies, come mostly because they realize this truth: tomorrow, and maybe even today, could bring the death of a loved one. Perhaps they notice how the grieving loved ones react, since they may have to answer death's knock someday.

The best way to beat death's sting is to take advantage of what today brings. With Marcie, we took advantage of so many great opportunities, but we still wish we could have had more days to celebrate the wonderful gift of her life. Today is your day. Tomorrow is not promised. Don't miss a moment; make every second count!

A beautiful embrace that I will always treasure—Me and Marcie, 2002

Julie, Robert, Vee, and Marcie
by Julie Arnold Erb

When Marcie died, I remember thinking, "Why Marcie?" She was the smartest, most talented person with such a unique spirit. She had so much to offer the world. And, selfishly, I felt like I needed her the most. But as the years have passed, I have developed a deep acceptance and thankfulness to God that it was Marcie, not Robert or Veronica. Robert and I did not get along as children. We needed time to repair what was damaged from our childhood. In our adulthood, Robert has become one of my best friends. During my divorce and as a single mother, Robert was the person I called on the most and who came when I needed help. And now, Robert is married to one of my best friends.

Veronica (Vee) was in seventh grade when Marcie died. She didn't have a full understanding of what had happened. I am sure she felt somewhat left out by the rest of the family's deep sadness and mourning. As an adult, Veronica has become the pillar of our family. She brings the most joy and fun to our gatherings. She is such a voice of reason and truly the best friend I have ever had. Veronica and I purposely chose to go to college close to home. Currently, the entire family lives within ten minutes of each other. Marcie's death brought our family together and taught us to cherish one another.

I have felt more pain in my life. When I chose to separate from and divorce my first husband, I told myself two things: first, this will never hurt as much as losing Marcie; Second, she would be in full support. A powerful question for me became: *Would Marcie want this for your life?* When I had my daughter, Maci, who was named after Marcie, I thought about how she would love her, and how proud she would be.

When I married Bryan, I knew Marcie would celebrate and understand that I had found my partner in life. I do feel Marcie's presence, from time to time, and I don't question it. Like Richard Rohr says in *"Everything Belongs"* (p. 199). Marcie's death *belonged* in the history of our family. The pain and blessings from losing her, continue to *belong*.

Julie & Bryan Erb's Wedding Day—August 12, 2017
Their children: Macie, Benjamin & Brinley

The Wisdom and Protection of the Owl

Once again, at a significant event in the life of our family, we heard from Marcie!

My daughter, Vee, was married in October of 2018 at the farm. The service and the reception were held at *Marcie's Meadow*. The day was incredible, and we sensed Marcie's presence. When I spoke of how Vee was so much like Marcie, the audience was in tears.

My wife Jeanne felt a deep sense of loss that Marcie was not able to be physically present. However, an amazing event occurred Monday morning after the wedding—just the encouragement that Jeanne needed!

I received the following message on Facebook, from someone I never knew, a young woman named Jennifer:

> *Hi, I know this may seem incredibly random, and I'm hoping I have the right person. I knew Marcie. I worked with her in Myrtle Beach. She's been on my mind a lot lately, and God laid it on my heart to reach out and tell you how much she meant to me. She was an incredible role model. She kept me out of trouble on numerous occasions; she always knew how to cheer me up; she was amazing at building up a person's confidence and making them feel loved. She was like a big sister to me.*
>
> *I have thought about her many times throughout the years, and we always thought it was so funny that my name was supposed to be Marcie Delane. Apparently, my parents didn't communicate it well and it ended up, Jennifer Renee. So we shared a middle name, but almost shared a first name, by nickname of course.*
>
> *Most importantly, I have no doubt that she planted seeds that led me to Christ so many years ago. I didn't find my new life in Christ until 2010, over a full decade after having met her. I couldn't tell you if we ever actually had a religious conversation, but there was something so loving, compassionate, forgiving, and full of grace about her that has always stuck with me, and really changed the way I have cared for people and ultimately, led me to pursue a relationship with Christ, and I am so very thankful for that.*
>
> *And I know this is so late, but I am so very sorry for your loss. Having children now, I can't possibly imagine what you went through, and continue to feel. I have prayed for your family*

*throughout the years and will continue to do so. I hope this message
finds you in good spirits and health.*

Over the next few days, I had an on-going discussion with
Marcie's friend, Jennifer, always a beautiful time. I sent her a
picture of *Marcie's Meadow* that my good friend Connell Byrne
had painted. Jennifer was very interested in why an owl was in
the picture.

Connell, who had passed away just months before the
wedding, had never told us why he painted an owl in the
picture. It was beautiful, but no one, not even his wife, Carol,
knew why he had included the owl.

I shared that with Jennifer and also mentioned a
conversation that I had a few weeks before the wedding with
the man who owns the property next to our farm. I had never
talked with him before, and he started by telling me that he
bought the land because it was so fertile. Then in passing, he
mentioned that the people who had owned the land earlier had
told him that whenever they drove into the property, owls
would accompany them up the road. Wow! What inspiration
Connell had received!

The story with Marcie's friend did not end there. She told
me that she had twins, and in their room was a picture of owls.
She said, "I've always loved foxes and owls. Bradford's room
got the fox, and the twins got the owls. It just caught me when
I saw the picture yesterday of the owl at the farm. I have always
seen the owl as a sign of a guardian." She went on to say, "I'm
predominantly Native American, and I was always told that
owls were a sign of protection."

This was so relevant to who Marcie was—a protector and,
sometimes, a rescuer. And like the owl, she had a wise soul.

Connell Byrne painted this beautiful acrylic and gave it to Jeanne and me in 2004. Later, in 2018, we had the painting replicated on a large metal sign. It sits prominently on the front gate of Marcie's Meadow.

Being Brave to Serve the Kingdom

"The brave are surely those who have the clearest vision of what is before them… And yet, go out to meet it." Thucydides

After losing Marcie, to just give up or quit seemed very easy. Many times, I wanted to stop fighting my grief and just give in and fade away. What I came to realize, however, was that this experience was making me stronger.

While giving up appeared to be much easier, I came to understand that the greatest of all spiritual service involves being willing to endure the deepest darkness for the sake of the Kingdom. God often asks: "Who would love me if I were not to bless? Would you? Who would walk through the unsightly places of life for me? Would you?" Growth, valor, courage, and service entails a willingness to walk into whatever and wherever God is calling.

Jesus says, "I will take care of you." God's highest motivation for bravery is not to receive benefit from it but for us, at any cost, to desire what God desires. One of the greatest descriptions I've read of bravery is reflected in these words by Thomas à Kempis, author of *The Imitation of Christ*

Who Would Be Willing to Serve God for Naught? by Thomas à Kempis[xxvii]

Jesus has many lovers of his Heavenly Kingdom, but few bearers of his cross. He has many desirous of comfort, but few of tribulation. All desire to rejoice with Him, but few are willing to endure anything for Him, or with Him. Many love Jesus, so long as adversity does not happen. O, how powerful the pure love of Jesus which is mixed with no self-interest or self-love! But they who love Jesus, for the sake of Jesus, and not for some special comfort of their own, bless Him: in all tribulation and anguish of heart, as well as in the state of highest comfort. And when he hath done all that is to be done, so far as he knoweth, let him think that he hath done nothing. Yet there is no man richer than he; no man more powerful, no man more free. For he can leave himself in the lowest place.

Why Am I Left Here?

From the moment that I came to know Christ and understand what heaven would be like. I understood that heaven would be a place where I wanted to spend my eternity. As C. S. Lewis expressed, "Heaven is the greatest party of all time. Its serious business is joy" (*Letters to Malcolm: Chiefly on Prayer*, pp. 92-93). When I am confronted with the choice of whether I am ready to leave for heaven, or not, I always and immediately choose heaven.

Marcie is in heaven; living in this great joy, enjoying all that I have dreamed of. Heaven is hers, and the serious business of heaven is her joy.

Yet, I am stuck here. Futility adds to despair. What is the purpose of life? Why all the pain? Why must we stay here, suffering, when we could all be in heaven? For it all just to end and join Marcie in eternal bliss makes more sense, for my family and me. How I wish we all could go to heaven to be with Marcie. That would seem to be the only possible ending of this difficult journey. And yet, I am here and probably will be for a long time. My children will be here even longer.

I know I am here to help Jeanne, Robert, Julie, and Vee cope with the considerable pain they feel. I can't abandon them in the midst of our great crisis. Because of all of them, right now, heaven is not my first option.

I began to imagine what Marcie, with her newfound perspective, would say. I think the conversation might go something like this:

Marcie: *"Dad, you were right! I wish I could have been more faithful to what I knew."*

Me: *"I wish I'd been more faithful to encourage you to follow him with all of your heart."*

Marcie: *"He is sooo good! He is sooo loving! This is what I have always desired."*

Me: *"I wish I could be with you."*

Marcie: *"Dad, you must stay. He wants you there. Take his words to the depths of your existence; trust them. He will take care of you and empower you. He desires, and needs, to use you for his honor and glory.*

Be even more faithful; dedicate 100% of yourself to his Kingdom! When you are prepared and ready, he will move!"

I have not revisited the question of why I was left here since 2003, until recently, when I was encouraged to write an update in this book about what God has done in my life since then.

Since Marcie's death, we held several Youth for Christ (YFC) conferences in Ocean City, Maryland for both middle school and high school students. In eleven years, we had over 72,000 in attendance, and made an amazing impact on thousands of middle and high school students and their leaders. Many students gave their lives to Christ at these conferences.

One of the most amazing experience for Jeanne and me during our years at YFC came in 2003. Our speaker, for the second time, was Darrell Scott, the father of Rachel Scott who had been murdered in 1999 during the Columbine High School shooting. Many thousands of students were impacted by Rachel's story and, later, made a difference in their schools. When listening to Darrell as he spoke to the students about his daughter's death, I realized that we now shared a common loss: the loss of a beautiful young daughters. I remember Darrell coming beside Jeanne and me and praying with us over the loss of Marcie. We became dear friends and remain friends to this day.

Over the remaining years we were privileged to host many outstanding youth speakers, including Steve Fitzhugh, Bob Lenz, Reggie Dabbs, and Joel Sonnenberg. We provided training for youth leaders, offering the best leadership trainers, including these: Brennan Manning, Ken Gire, Larry Crabb, Walt Muellar, Dave Rahn, and Hugh Ross. Several of these speakers became great friends that I continue to speak with today. We also hosted many excellent bands that played at these events. The bands brought the students and leaders into an amazing time of worship and community. As a result of these events, thousands of students came to know and follow Christ!

In addition to those events, we led an annual ski retreat for youth called *Living End* and had summer retreats at the beach. We, also, held yearly golf tournament led by Ben Renko, which raised thousands of dollars for our ministry.

We hosted an annual Baltimore area-wide fundraising banquet that began to be a major event for the Christian community. My friend, Grant Grasmick, spearheaded the event, and throughout the next ten years, we had over 10,000 people in attendance, and raised over $3,000,000 for Metro-Maryland YFC.

My friends from YFC, Joel Smith and Howard Lucy, began a leadership training event at our family farm, Marcie's Meadow, which became known as *The Forum*. Over a nine-year period, we hosted 36 students, and provided some of the best speakers and leaders for training in spiritual leadership. Groups of twelve people would meet three times a year for three years. Many were led to become major leaders in the YFC organization.

After all these activities, I began to wear out. In 2013, I retired from YFC and followed God's leading. Jeanne and I began a new ministry called *The Meadow*. It encourages people to walk deeper with the Lord. We are now blessed to focus our ministry on those who face difficult life situations and who desire to know God and his overwhelming love in greater ways to carry them through.

Jeanne and I are so humbled to have been given more years to continue to serve God's Kingdom and to serve others. *"For we are God's handiwork, created in Christ Jesus to do good works, which God prepared in advance for us to do"* (Ephesians. 2:10).

To the Generations That Follow
... and to Those Who Have Shared This Journey

A very holy moment happened in the history of our family. Sharing our story, following the loss of our Marcie, has taken me 17 years. Since Marcie, "the Reborn Anvil," had such a short time on this earth, so many did not get to know her. So, I wanted you to become acquainted with Marcie and her story. I want her to always be remembered in the history of our family and our friends. I hope our reflections of Marcie's life and death will shape and mold our family's future generations to become the great people that God intends.

If you have faced the sorrowful loss of a child, I hope our story will bring comfort and support. Sorrow is not an overnight experience but one that becomes a part of who we are and who we will become. Seeing the similarities of our sorrow with yours may help you navigate this dark road. I so much want you to know that God cares and understands your deepest pain and that he is always as near as your breath. My heart's longing is for you to know that God desires to walk in this deep darkness side-by-side with you and for you to know that he has felt, in the very deepest sense, all of the pain and the anguish that you feel.

The deepest healing comes from God, who will find us in the midst of our pain and woundedness. Although all our journeys of sorrow are unique, our healing can help so many others who are suffering. I have seen it, time and time again personally, and saw I it in the with others. Our suffering became joy, not the joy of singing and dancing, but the joy of God's presence and of helping others in the midst of their suffering. Our suffering can bring us a powerful strength that will surprise us with gifts that surpass any understanding. By the strength that God provides, stand emboldened to embrace the *deep sorrow*, and be encouraged to savor the surprising joy!

My Journey with Cancer
A Newfound Inspiration

The telling of our almost two-decade journey, following the loss of our daughter Marcie, has not ended our suffering. But walking through the suffering with God has enhanced our living and our dedication to love others as Christ has loved us.

The healing, strength, and courage that God has given to me over these many years has helped me through other times of suffering. Life can change in the blink of an eye, and we never seem to be fully prepared, but, rest assured, God is walking with us, and providing others to help us along our journey.

Most recently, I had a battle with cancer. In January of 2019, I was diagnosed with an aggressive form of prostate cancer.

When I received the news, I began an inner journey of what having cancer means. Initially told, I was in a state of shock. My first thoughts were that perhaps I had done all that I would be able to do in my lifetime. Considering the real possibility of death followed, and I thought maybe that would not be so bad. I had lived a good life. I would go on to join my many friends and beloved daughter, Marcie. On the surface, the prospect seemed exciting.

That began to change. At first, I decided to share my battle with others and receive the affirmation I thought I needed— but God thought otherwise. I felt led to keep this a private issue among him, Jeanne, and myself. In the days that followed, I was able to spend countless periods of time with God, receiving his compassion and care.

I began to pray and contemplate what I needed to do to be cured. My doctor recommended surgery.

The doctor was able to remove the cancer, except for some that had overflowed to nearby tissue. Later in the year, I underwent radiation treatment to eradicate the remaining cancer cells.

Over the last few months, I have spent a great deal of time contemplating and praying through the many emotional and spiritual issues of life after cancer. Suffering is an emotional and spiritual battle, but I became aware of a newly formed perspective created by my suffering.

I have an enhanced perspective that gives me a new look at life. We know that life is short, but when confronted with one's own death, we have a deeper insight into our frailty.

I did not suffer from a sense that my life was wasted and that I needed to make up for all that was lost. Just the opposite was true. I felt tremendous gratitude for how God had rescued my life and had given me a great vision to work for his kingdom and make a difference in the others' lives.

The words in 2 Corinthians 1:3–7 have never rung more true: *Praise be to the God and Father of our Lord Jesus Christ, the Father of compassion and the God of all comfort, who comforts us in all our troubles, so that we can comfort those in any trouble, with the comfort we ourselves receive from God. For just as we share abundantly in the sufferings of Christ, so also our comfort abounds through Christ.*

My battle with cancer is now behind me. I realize now that God has given me time to focus on this book during my illness. I was able to quietly and purposefully look back at my journals with a new objective. The desire to write this book was always there, but enough time and resources never seemed to exist. God provided both during this last year, and I am forever grateful.

As Jeanne and I move into the next years of our lives, we see it as a time to pursue a deeper walk in the depths of God's love and to bring hope to people going through life's sufferings and sorrow. We long to inspire people to experience God in a more intimate and personal way while knowing the great depths of his love. We thank God for our family and friends, as well as our ministry of *The Meadow*. We look forward to continuing to use our gifts to inspire people to embrace God's love and compassion, sharing that with the world around them. We passionately encourage everyone to continue to enrich their relationship with Jesus Christ. He is the ultimate giver of all comfort, peace, and joy. God is STILL (and always) good. God is STILL (and always) faithful. God is STILL (and always) loving!

Our family at Vee and Scott's wedding in Marcie's Meadow October 6, 2017

From left to right (Back Row) Robert Jr. Jeanne, me, Veronica and Scott Bracken, Julie and Bryan Erb (Front Row) Julie and Bryan's children, Brinley, Macie, and Benjamin.

Our son's wedding in Baltimore, MD, Nora and Robert, Jr., June 1, 2019

From left to right:
(Back Row) Bryan and Julie, Jeanne, Nora, and Robert Jr., me, and
Scott (Front Row) Benjamin, Brinley, Macie, Vee, and Jeanne's
mother, Dorothy Certeza.

ACKNOWLEDGEMENTS

I want to personally thank my wife Jeanne, my children, my many friends, and those who have shared their intimate stories within these pages. I have been encouraged by so many to write this book, and I am truly blessed to have been able to give life to this story on paper. My desire has been to honor my daughter Marcie's life, and through everyone's help I have been able to fulfill this dream.

Writing this book can be compared to the story of Tom Sawyer when he was made to whitewash his Aunt's fence as a punishment for playing hooky from school. Completing this whole job alone would have been a daunting task, but Tom, being the great encourager, convinced his friends that the work was not tedious but was, in fact, a great privilege and even an honor to paint the fence. His friends not only jumped into paint but also enjoyed helping him.

My story somewhat compares to Tom Sawyer in that when many friends heard I was writing this story, they wanted to help me in any way they could. My family and friends contributed greatly to the completion of my original efforts. They brought my many meditations together and made it a beautiful project!

The first friend I would like to thank is Maria Avery. When I expressed my desire to write this book, Maria offered to help edit and organize my original 75 chapters. Without her countless hours of help, this project would have never begun.

When the first draft was completed, we had several copies beautifully bound and printed by Dave Adams. Seeing the book in a readable format made me very eager to get it published; however, my good friend Donna Martin convinced me otherwise. She championed the project with a newfound sense of organization. She researched guidelines for writing and set timelines for polishing the book into its final copy.

Donna and I organized a group of friends to begin an extensive editing process, among them Edie Bernier, Kenny Lee, Kelly Greco, Matt Paavola and Randy Martin. My wife Jeanne, my dear friends Roy and Barbara Sleeman, along with Randy, Donna, Maria, and Edie, spent three nights together reading the book aloud and providing feedback. I also can't forget Helen Martin who contributed her graphic skills to the book's cover. To all my friends who took the many meditations and transformed them into a work of beauty, I thank you!

I would also like to acknowledge my precious friend, Bev Gorman, who wrote two chapters in the book: *The Pietà* and *Marcie Renee Arnold—Her Eulogy*. To this day they still reflect so much of what we felt at the time of Marcie's death. Her words captured the very essence of our experience.

The stories shared by other friends about their personal experiences with grief have become some of the most important parts of this book. They are especially beneficial to those of us walking through the valley of sorrow. Many thanks to these writers: Tim Price, Grant Grasmick, John and Tee Kelly, Nancy Fallace, Stuart Pierce, Howard Lucy, and Dr. Ian MacFawn and Cathy MacFawn. And thanks to Glenda and Walter Ziatek and Jeff Elkins for their encouragement.

Most importantly I want to thank my beautiful family, Jeanne my wife of 42 years, and my wonderful children, Robert, Julie, and Veronica "Vee." From the moment we first learned about Marcie's death, our family has walked side-by-side in our sadness and mourning. Together in our deep sorrow, we have been able to help each other grow closer as a family and discover our surprising joy.

This book is truly a labor of love from my family and the many people who knew Marcie and have loved us for so many years!

Resources and Additional Reading Suggestions

A Grace Disguised
by Jerry Sittser
Publisher: Zondervan; Revised edition (December 28, 2004)
ISBN-10: 0310266149 - ISBN-13: 978-0310266143

A Grief Observed
by C. S. Lewis (Author), Madeleine L'Engle (Foreword)
Publisher: HarperOne; first edition (February 6, 2001)
ISBN-10: 0060652381 - ISBN-13: 978-0060652388

A Grief Sanctified (Including Richard Baxter's Timeless
Memoir of His Wife's Life and Death):

Through Sorrow to Eternal Hope
by J. I. Packer (Author), Richard Baxter (Contributor)
Publisher: Crossway (September 24, 2002)
ISBN-10: 1581344406 - ISBN-13: 978-1581344400

**A Grief Unveiled: One Father's Journey Through the
Loss of a Child**
by Gregory Floyd (Author), Thomas Howard (Foreword)
Publisher: Paraclete Press (May 1, 1999)
ISBN-10: 1557252157 - ISBN-13: 978-1557252159

**A Time of Departing: How ancient mystical practices are
uniting Christians with the world's religions**
by Ray Yungen
Publisher: Lighthouse Trails Publishing, Inc.; 2nd edition
(May 8, 2020)
ISBN-10: 0972151273 - ISBN-13: 978-0972151276

A Voice in the Wilderness
by Joseph Bayly (Author), Timothy B. Bayly (Editor)
Publisher: David C. Cook; New edition (January 3, 2000)
ISBN-10: 1564767876 - ISBN-13: 978-1564767875

Dark Clouds Deep Mercy
by Mark Vroegop
Publisher: Crossway (March 21, 2019)
ISBN-10: 1433561484 - ISBN-13: 978-143356148

Exploring Heaven: What Great Christian Thinkers Tell Us About Our Afterlife with God
by Arthur O. Roberts
Publisher: HarperSanFrancisco; 1 edition (August 1, 2003)
ISBN-10: 0060530685 - ISBN-13: 978-0060530686

Finding Purpose in Your Pain
by V. Gilbert Beers
Publisher: Fleming H Revell Co; Reprint edition (March 1, 1998)
ISBN-10: 0800786491 - ISBN-13: 978-0800786496

Hammers & Nails: The Life and Music of Mark Heard
by Matthew T Dickerson
Publisher: Cornerstone Press Chicago (May 2003)
ISBN-10: 0940895501 - ISBN-13: 978-0940895508

Holding onto Hope: A Pathway through Suffering to the Heart of God
by Nancy Guthrie (Author), Anne Graham Lotz (Foreword)
Publisher: Tyndale Momentum (November 1, 2006)
ISBN-13 : 978-1414312965 - ASIN: B001ELJV4K

Lament for a Son
by Nicholas Wolterstorff (Author)
Publisher: Eerdmans; 1 edition (May 18, 1987)
ISBN-10: 080280294X - ISBN-13: 978-0802802941

Living Through Personal Crisis
by Ann Kaiser Stearns
Publisher: Idyll Arbor; 2nd edition (May 5, 2010)
ISBN-10: 9781882883875 - ISBN-13: 978-1882883875 - ASIN: 188288387X

Making Sense Out of Suffering
by Peter Kreeft
Publisher: Servant; Second Printing edition (July 1, 1986)
ISBN-10: 0892832193 - ISBN-13: 978-0892832194

On Death and Dying (Scribner Classics) Classic edition
by M.D. Elisabeth Kubler-Ross
Publisher: Scribner Classics; Later Edition (1997)
ASIN: B01182EQ5S

Preparing for Heaven: What Dallas Willard Thinks about Living,
Dying and Eternal Life
By Gary Black Jr.
Publisher: HarperOne (October 13, 2015)
ISBN-10: 9780062365521 - ISBN-13: 978-0062365521

Rachel's Tears: 10th Anniversary Edition: The Spiritual
Journey of Columbine Martyr Rachel Scott
by Beth Nimmo (Author), Darrell Scott (Author), Steve Rabey
(Contributor)
Publisher: Thomas Nelson; 10th Anniversary ed. edition
(February 16, 2009)
ISBN-10: 1400313473 - ISBN-13: 978-1400313471

Rare Bird: A Memoir of loss and love
By Anna Whiston-Donaldson
Publisher: Convergent Books; Reprint edition (September 8,
2015)
ISBN-10: 160142520 - ISBN-13: 978-1601425201

Recovering from Losses in Life
by H. Norman Wright
Publisher: Revell (June 18, 2019)
ISBN-10: 0800736001 - ISBN-13: 978-0800736002

Sing Me to Heaven: The Story of a Marriage
by Margaret Kim Peterson
Publisher: Brazos Press (August 1, 2003)
ISBN-10: 1587430479 - ISBN-13: 978-1587430473

Streams in The Dessert
by L. B. Cowman (Author), James Reimann (Author)
Publisher: Zondervan; Revised edition (June 1, 1999)
ISBN-10: 0310210062 - ISBN-13: 978-0310210061

Tender Fingerprints
by Brad Stetson
Publisher: Zondervan (September 1, 1999)
ISBN-10: 0310228670 - ISBN-13: 978-0310228677

The Denial of Death
by Ernest Becker
Publisher: Free Press; 1 edition (May 8, 1997)

ISBN-10: 0684832402 - ISBN-13: 978-0684832401

The Last Dance: Encountering Death and Dying
by Lynne Ann DeSpelder (Author), Albert Lee Strickland
(Author)
Publisher: McGraw-Hill Education; 10th edition (March 28, 2014)
ISBN-10: 0078035465 - ISBN-13: 978-0078035463

The Last Thing We Talk About: Help and Hope for Those Who Grieve
by Joseph Bayly
Publisher: Chariot Family Pub; Updated edition (June 1, 1992)
ISBN-10: 0781400481 - ISBN-13: 978-0781400480

The Lively Shadow: Living with the Death of a Child
by Donald M. Murray
Publisher: Ballantine Books; 1st edition (February 4, 2003)
ISBN-10: 0345449843 - ISBN-13: 978-0345449849

Turn My Mourning into Dancing: Finding Hope in Hard Times
by Henri Nouwen
Publisher: Thomas Nelson (June 29, 2004)
ISBN-10: 0849945097 - ISBN-13: 978-0849945090

We Never Said Goodbye
by Dr. R. L. Wright
ISBN-10: 1556304765 - ISBN-13: 978-1556304767

What You Should Know About Life after Death: Life After Death
by Dr. Spiros Zodhiates
Publisher: AMG Publishers; Revised edition (January 1, 2002)
ISBN-10: 0899575250 - ISBN-13: 978-0899575254

When Children Grieve: For Adults to Help Children Deal with Death, Divorce, Pet Loss, Moving, and Other Losses
by John W. James (Author), Russell Friedman (Author), Leslie Matthews (Author)
Publisher: Harper Perennial; Reprint edition (June 4, 2002)

ISBN-10: 9780060084295 - ISBN-13: 978-0060084295 -
ASIN: 0060084294

When God Weeps: Why Our Sufferings Matter to the Almighty
by Joni Eareckson Tada
Publisher: Zondervan (June 22, 2010) - Sold by HarperCollins
Publishing
ISBN-10: 0310238358 - ISBN-13: 978-0310238355
ASIN: B003OYIA3I

When the Bough Breaks: Forever After the Death of a Son or Daughter
by Ph.D. Judith R. Bernstein
Publisher: Andrews McMeel Publishing; Original ed. edition
(March 3, 1998)
ISBN-10: 0836252829 - ISBN-13: 978-0836252828

When Your Father Dies: How a Man Deals with the Loss of His Father
by Dave Veerman and Bruce B. Barton
Publisher: Thomas Nelson Inc (September 5, 2006)
ISBN-10: 0785288309 - ISBN-13: 978-0785288305

The Pietà

(Italian: [pje'ta]; English: "The Pity"; 1498–1499) is a work of Renaissance sculpture by Michelangelo Buonarroti, housed in St. Peter's Basilica, Vatican City. - Wikipedia 2020 ©

Michelangelo's Pietà in
St. Peter's Basilica, Vatican City.
(wikipedia CC BY 3.0)

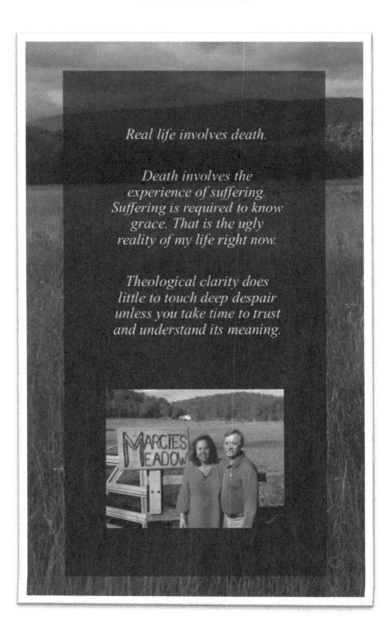

Real life involves death.

Death involves the
experience of suffering.
Suffering is required to know
grace. That is the ugly
reality of my life right now.

Theological clarity does
little to touch deep despair
unless you take time to trust
and understand its meaning.

Endnotes

ⁱ Mercy Me, *I Can Only Imagine*, Artist, Mercy Me Album: The Worship Project, released 1999.

ⁱⁱ J. Frank Wilson, *Last Kiss*, Artist: J. Frank Wilson and Cavaliers; Album: Last Kiss, released 1964.

ⁱⁱⁱ Ken Gire, *The Work of His Hands,* Vine Books, 2002

^{iv} Wanda Bencke, "My First Christmas in Heaven," © 1992, 1997, 1998.

^v John Eldridge, *Waking the Dead,* Thomas Nelson Publishers, Nashville, TN, general theme, © 2006.

^{vi} C.S. Lewis, *A Grief Observed,* HarperCollins Publishers, page 1; © 1992.

^{vii} Richard Rohr, *The Mystery of Suffering,* Crossroad Publishers, quoted on Rohr's email, January 24, 2018 © 1998.

^{viii} Fr. Iain Matthew, *The Impact of God,* Hodder & Stoughton, Chapter 15 & 16, The Experience of God; © 1995)

^{ix} *Teresa of Avila on Suffering.* Cambridge University Press, p.75. "I Desire to Suffer, Lord, because Thou didst Suffer"; Hypatia, Cambridge Core, Cambridge University Press.

^x Fred Rogers, *You Are Special: Neighborly Wit and Wisdom from Mister Rogers. Running Press; Min Edition* ©2002

^{xi} Nicholas Woltersdorf, *Lament for a Son.* Eerdmans Publishers, © 1987, page 80.

^{xii} Ernest Becker, *The Denial of Death*, Free Press, pages 11-14, © 1997.

^{xiii} Anne Lamont, *Traveling Mercies,* Anchor Publishers, page 239, © Feb 2000 edition.

^{xiv} Maggie Callanan and Patricia Kelley, *Thoughts from the Diary of a Desperat Man: A Daily Deotional.* February 3, 1997.

^{xv} Dallas Willard and Gary Black Jr., *Preparing for Death,* HarperOne Publishers, page 254, ©2015.

^{xvi} Joe Bayly, *The View from a Hearse: A Christian View of Death,* David C. Cook Publishing, © 1969)

^{xvii} "The Long Goodbye" Artist: Brooks & Dunn. Album: Steers & Stripes, 2001.

^{xviii} Ranier Maria Rilke, *Letters to a Young Priest.* Merchant Books, © 2012.

xix Nancy Guthrie, *Holding On to Hope,* Tyndale Momentum, page 82, © 2015.

xx *The Wisdom of the Cherokee,* Tsalagi Tale

xxi Jean-Pierre de Caussade, *The Sacrament of the Present Moment.* Createspace, 2013.

xxii C.S. Lewis, *The Screwtape Letters,* HarperOne reprint edition, 2015, Chapter XV.

xxiii Iain Matthew, page 167

xxiv Ibid, page 171

xxv No source found, widely quoted.

xxvi Donald Murray, *The Lively Shadow,* Ballantine Books, 2003, page 193.

xxvii Thomas a Kempis, *The Imitation of Christ, Chapter 36.*